Parents and Teachers

A

Acknowledgements

I could not have written this book without the help and encouragement of many people, parents, teachers and those who are both. Their number runs into hundreds, but I would be ungrateful if I did not mention the enthusiastic assistance of Kay and Ronald Aldridge, Peter Bensley, Richard Blake, Jean Hales, Michael Harris, Kathleen Hartley, D. D. Mackay, Deborah Martin, Patrick McGeeney, Emily Russell, Pamela Schaub, Harry and Joan Stephenson, Vanda Stephenson, Gertrude Thurman, A. Roy Truman, Frances Walton and Michael Young.

I received generous help from my employer, the Inner London Education Authority, but they are in no way responsible for my opinions or for the book's conclusions.

Above all, the book would not have seen the light of day without the constant support of my wife, Jean, whose strong belief in the value of home-school co-operation has enabled me to devote so much of my out-of-school time to this study.

Preface

BY MICHAEL YOUNG
*Chairman, Home and School Council and
member, Plowden Committee*

SOCIAL change is said to be slower in Britain than anywhere else in the world. The advocates of change often seem to be speaking to themselves in a private echo chamber; to be only too effective, their opponents do not need to do more than pretend not to hear them. That was, I would say, about where we were with parent-teacher relations ten years ago. A few pioneers, like Mr Green himself, were demonstrating what could be done in city schools. They were trying to repeat in cities what had happened quite naturally in many village schools (and in a very few exceptional city ones) for a very long time. In rural areas parents and teachers were often at one because they belonged to a community which was a community in more than name. But the pioneers had few followers. 'No Parents Beyond This Line' still expressed the common attitude.

Since then the mood has begun to alter. This does not easily happen in England but when it does the change is very obvious. The white lines in the playgrounds have begun to disappear. Some of the old notices by the gates saying 'Parents Not Allowed Beyond This Point' have been taken down. Parents are actually figuring in the curriculum of colleges of education. In a few of them, as well as in a few universities, teacher social workers are being trained for the express purpose of maintaining liaison with parents. There are more in-service courses on parents for teachers, and the first few for teachers and parents together. The last of the three reports of the sixties from the Central Advisory Council for Education, the Plowden Report, made its main theme the need to take parents into partnership with teachers. In more and more schools teachers are taking trouble to communicate with parents instead of leaving it just to chance. I would say it is already clear that for the future no young teacher will be appointed to a headship unless he can show that he has tried and succeeded in this art of communication, to adults as well as to their children. Why all this has happened in mid-century I do not think anyone yet knows; but that it has happened, and is happening, can now hardly be denied.

The mood has changed. What is now needed most of all is know-how. The time is past for fine appeals for 'better' parent-teacher relations. We, and by 'we' I mean both the parties to the education of children, now need to get down to brass tacks, and decide just what can be done in practice to give effect to the new mood. In this task Mr Green is one of the best guides we could have. He has done it in his own school. He speaks with authority; and he speaks about the details which, added one to another from Mr Green's school and many others, are in the next ten years going to introduce a new tradition to the schools of a country where tradition is important.

Contents

CHAPTER 1

'No Parents Beyond This Line'

You are taking your child to school for the first time. As you enter the school gate you see other mothers. They seem to have arranged themselves in a rough line facing the school. The head teacher appears on the steps. A ripple of movement passes through the group and you see that there *is* a line—it is painted on the playground. Below it is a message, probably your first communication from the school. It reads, 'No parents beyond this line.'

This is not fantasy but fact. It happened in September 1966. The school concerned is in a city administered by a progressive education authority whose official policy it is to encourage all forms of contact between home and school.

On the same day, in the same city, there were many schools where parents and their children were welcomed. Despite small classrooms and large numbers of children, despite the teachers' not knowing the Greek or Urdu words for 'Welcome,' parents were, in these other schools, made to feel that they were not unwelcome intruders.

But how typical is the line painted on the playground? And how typical, and meaningful, the welcome? The line, however infuriating to some parents, is at least honest. It means, 'You've brought them to school now. Don't fuss over them. Leave them with us, we're the experts. It's kindest to make a clean break.'

Infant schools in many places invite parents to see them at work before their children enrol. Some encourage pupils to bring younger brothers and sisters, who are not of statutory age, for an occasional visit. Where a nursery school is attached to a primary school it is a simple and obvious step to introduce the under-5s to the over-5s and so make the beginning of school less of an ordeal.

But nursery schools are pitifully few and far between. 'There were less than 500 nursery schools in the country, most of them taking not more than fifty children.' (Mrs. G. R. Osborn, Chairman, National Council of Women education sectional committee, in a speech at the N.C.W. annual conference, Harrogate, October 1966).

Efforts are being made in some junior schools to provide greater opportunity for contact with parents. It is becoming standard practice to consult parents, by means of an interview, on their wishes for the child's secondary education. And in the secondary schools themselves parents can discuss with careers teachers the prospects open to school-leavers, though Brian Jackson and Dennis Marsden in the *Education and the Working Class*[1] have shown how bewildered and frustrated many such parents are and how few are the opportunities for extended discussion between parents of teenage children and the teachers having expert knowledge of career prospects. *Education and the Working Class* was concerned with a small number of grammar school leavers and their subsequent careers in higher education. But such was the nature of its findings, and so disturbing its analysis of the failure of schools to communicate, that its publication in 1962 caused repercussions throughout the whole field of education.

It says of parents: ' . . . what they reported and resented was the meagre opportunity of seeing teachers, and the irrelevance of the comment and advice they did receive. The last things they desired were sharp little pep-talks urging their child to work even harder.'[2]

The line is still there. It is not often painted on the playground. But it is there wherever the teachers think or say—

[1] *Education and the Working Class.* London, Routledge and Kegan Paul, 1962.
[2] *op. cit.* p. 118.

and they often do say with the best intentions 'Leave them to us. They'll be all right. We know best.'

It is the central theme of this book that there is not enough contact between parents and teachers, that far too many parents feel frustrated and annoyed by the lack of consultation and communication, that even where means of communication exist they are not used or are used unimaginatively, which means ineffectively. Above all, and in this personal opinion based on sixteen years as a teacher and eleven as a parent I know I am supported by very many people, parents often feel that what they want for their own child is somehow in conflict with what the head teacher wants for the school as a whole.

I hasten to add that my teaching experience, all of it in schools built before 1900 in what may be described as 'deprived' areas, has given me the greatest admiration for the teaching profession. With overlarge classes, with inadequate buildings, with salaries which would be laughed at in industry, teachers have nevertheless succeeded in educating our children. Further, large numbers of them give freely of their spare time to serve the community through the children. Football and cricket, Saturday mornings at the Tower of London or the museums, music and drama in the evenings, school fortnights at the seaside or in the country—in all these activities, and in many more, teachers give generously.

To criticise the lack of real contact between home and school is not simply to criticise teachers. When you as a young teacher are responsible for forty-two eleven-year-old children in a junior school it needs a highly developed understanding of the real importance of good contact with parents before you give up the evening job which you do, to bring your net salary over the £12 a week margin, in order to visit pupils' homes!

One of the few investigations into parent-teacher contact was that undertaken by Political and Economic Planning.[3] Their

[3] *Parents' Views on Education*, London, P.E.P. 1961, pp. 17-26.

results, published in 1961 in the booklet, *Parents' Views on Education,* are disturbing. Mothers of 734 families in the Greater London area were interviewed about their experience of the education service.

The analysis shows that:

Only 8% selected education as the social service that had helped their family most.

42% felt they did not know enough of their child's school and wished to know more.

35% felt they were not told enough about what went on at their children's schools.

The report adds, 'In general there was most criticism of primary and secondary modern schools and least criticism of grammar, technical and private schools. About a third of the mothers with children at junior schools commented critically on a school in this category. It was junior schools that came in for most criticism.'

The second theme of this book is that a great deal of what we try to do in the schools is wasted because we have too little understanding of our pupils' environment. Some of us tend to see the school as an island of culture in a sea of barbarism. Our speech, our dress, our values, set us apart from our pupils and their homes. We do not usually live where they live. 'All some of us know of the neighbourhood is the quickest way to the nearest bus stop,' as one Headmaster said to me. There are few 'Miss Reads' and no village schools in Stepney, Salford or Smethwick.

I am not advocating that we teachers should all move into the 'deprived' areas, drop our *h*s and give our pupils a diet of the Rolling Stones for music, Bingo for mathematics and comics for English appreciation. What I am urging is that, especially in the less favoured areas of our big cities, teachers should be encouraged to get to know the areas around the schools, to see the problems parents have to grapple with, and

14

to incorporate in their teaching what they learn. Encouraged? By what means? This is for the community, not just the teachers, to decide.

Encouragement could mean special financial inducements to attract teachers to such areas—but our profession is plagued and divided enough already by special allowances on top of an inadequate basic salary. However, the Crowther Committee recommended that 'in the bad areas, which pay much more than their fair share of the price for a shortage of teachers, there should be an attempt to discover by experiment whether financial incentives to teachers to serve in difficult areas would be effective.' (*15 to 18*. Vol. 1, p. 471.) The recent Plowden Report recommends, 'As a matter of national policy "positive discrimination" should favour schools in neighbour- hoods where children are most severely handicapped by home conditions. The programme should be phased to make schools in the most deprived areas as good as the best of the country. For this it may be necessary that their greater claim on resources should be maintained'.[4] It should mean the speeding- up of slum clearance and the planning of new schools as parts of communities where teachers would live. It should mean a much greater emphasis in teacher training on the *social* role of the school and the teacher. It should also mean, and here parents can play a part, that teachers are welcomed in a community and made to feel that they are valued members. It *may* mean the schools must help create the community.

In any case, the problem is not just concerned with schools in deprived areas. In some ways, as the experiment described later on shows, parents in such areas are more willing to accept help from the schools when it is offered because they need it so much more.

Is it an exaggeration to speak of widespread frustration among parents at lack of contact with their children's schools?

[4] *Children and their Primary Schools,* Vol. 1, pp. 464-5.

15

Is the school untypical which views every parent as a distraction, if not a potential nuisance who wants only to ask about her child's prospect of a place in grammar school or university?

'Tell your mother she's not to call at school' was the title of an article in the national Sunday newspaper, *The Observer*, on June 2, 1963. It was from a woman who was surprised to find that, when she moved to southern England, it was made plain to her at her child's school that she could not just 'drop in,' have a few words with the class teacher, and look at her child's books. She asked if this was typical. The next week the newspaper was inundated with letters on the subject. Many were from teachers, couched in not very temperate language. One described the lady's letter as 'cool effrontery'. Another asked, 'Would it be the 11-plus she has in mind?' Others made it plain that parents were a nuisance—teachers should be left alone to get on with their job. 'Get to hell out of it' was how one teacher forcibly put it!

There were also many letters from parents. A few described relations with schools which were happy and fruitful. But more echoed the original writer and complained that parents were given forcibly the feeling that they should be seen and not heard. For example 'At the primary school attended by my child it seems that any interest or concern on the part of a parent is regarded as interfering. The idea of a parent-teacher association has been greeted with horror and it has been made clear that any contribution by the parent is bound to be harmful—except for a monetary one towards a swimming pool.'

This is not an isolated instance. Local newspapers often publish similar sets of letters. Sometimes a parent will put, or try to understand, the teacher's point of view. Or a teacher will deplore the attitude of regarding parents as 'Public enemy number one.' Members of parent-teacher associations, unfortunately far too few in number, will sometimes describe the ways in which both 'sides' are getting together. But only too

16

often these local controversies reveal the wide gaps which exist.

Another unhappy example was the recent case of a mother keeping her child from school because the school forbade the use of a serviette to wipe cutlery, and magistrates removed the child from the mother as a result. (I am not passing an opinion on the case but citing it as an extreme example of what happens when real communication is lacking).

The case was the subject of much discussion among parents who saw it as one more example of the high-handed behaviour of head teachers and their arbitrary rules. Once more the correspondence columns of newspapers printed letters from irate parents. A few applauded the action of the magistrates. But most did not. It was clear that many of the writers resented the type of control exercised over children by head teachers. School uniforms and edicts on hairstyles came in for much criticism. It emerged too that what parents resented were the censorious remarks often addressed to children yet recognised by all concerned as reflecting on parents.

One mother recounted her experience in an interview with a head teacher. Her child had eye trouble. When she took him to school after a visit to the clinic the head said to the child, in the mother's presence, 'Well, if you will stay up all hours watching television.'

What was disconcerting, and, to those of us who are trying to develop co-operation, discouraging, was the view commonly held that the school is part of the hierarchy of law and order.

Teachers, or at least head teachers, were seen as part of 'they'—authority, that is. An untrue picture, and an unfair one? I think so. But it is a view still held and much more widely than generally supposed.

The basic problem, I feel, is one of communication. Most schools, it could be demonstrated, are doing an effective job. Only a minority—even if a large one—of parents are actively dissatisfied. Yet do the effective schools manage to display

17

their effectiveness to the parents, to convince them of it? Do the satisfied parents see the need to express their satisfaction? and have they the means by which to do it? Many schools have 'crossed the line', have moved from not telling parents to telling parents. A few, too few, have moved from telling parents to telling parents *why*.

The following is a simple example of lack of communication. A parent received a note from a head teacher a few months ago. It read: 'All classes in the Junior School will be dismissed at 3.45 p.m. (instead of 4 p.m.) all next week, Monday, 7th February—Friday 11th February.' Apart from the name of the school and the head's name, nothing. In discussion with other mystified parents she learnt that the local paper had mentioned a series of courses which teachers were to attend. The parents assumed this was the reason for the early closure. Some of them had to leave work earlier or to make special arrangements for their children to be minded. When they knew the reason for the change they appreciated it. But it was only by accident that they found out.

This was at least an advance on not being told. The same parent had previously had a most frustrating experience. Her nine-year-old was due for a two-day mid-term holiday. She said to the child, 'Well, you'll be on holiday on Monday and Tuesday.' 'Oh no,' said the child, 'we've got the whole week off!' The mother thereupon wrote to the school asking for written confirmation. The school was one whose phone number was not listed; there was no reply.

Schools have many problems. They cannot be expected to issue a constant stream of information without a much more generous measure of secretarial help. What industrial or commercial undertaking with 300 workers would expect to run efficiently if its secretary worked only in the morning, its managing director typed his own letters and could not meet visitors because he was attending to someone's bleeding nose,

18

his board having decided it was not worth while employing a nurse?

However friendly parents feel towards a school it is with some measure of trepidation that they entrust their child to its care.

Parents want their children to grow up, to be independent, but they want to share in their education. They want to pass on values, attitudes, feelings. If they believe in co-operation they do not want their children to be lined up for the rat-race. If they believe in equality of opportunity they do not want their children streamed, even if they get into the A stream.

When the school's philosophy coincides with theirs they still want to participate. It is impossible in any case to prevent parents helping to educate. The question is, can they be influenced to educate along the lines the school is using?

More and more teachers would answer 'Yes.' Parents' attitudes—of hostility, suspicion, antagonism—can be changed or at least improved, as I hope later chapters will show. This can be done not simply by telling but by telling *why*.

Is it only parents' attitudes that need changing? I think not. In many libraries books on home-school relations are classified under the heading 'Parent Education.' In fact the admirable survey by H. H. Stern for UNESCO is called *Parent Education —An International Survey*. (This survey reveals that England is behind such countries as Poland, Turkey and Yugoslavia in organised parent-teacher contact!) But contact between parents and teachers enables *both* to learn. As Dr Stern writes, about the term 'parent education':

'This concept which places parents in the passive role of a pupil who receives lessons from the teacher, and lends itself to the interpretation that they have everything to learn from the school, does not correspond to what is happening at present nor to what we should like to happen in the future. We prefer the term "Co-operation between Parents and

19

Teachers," which raises parents to the level of the teacher and makes them active participants'.[5]

We have to move one further stage: as well as telling parents, we tell them why. As well as telling them why, let us *ask* them sometimes. Cannot the most gifted, experienced teacher learn something from Mr and Mrs Smith who have brought up three children in three rooms, always sending them to school on time, adequately dressed, neat and cheerful? And how many teachers still, in the words of one head teacher, 'Adopt a boxer's defensive crouch when they see a parent coming?'

The means of communication are at hand. Not enough of them, it is true. Parent-teacher associations and parents' associations exist, but in a small minority of schools. These PTAs do immensely valuable work, and I feel that no real advance in solving the problems of communication between home and school is possible until there are far more of them. But a PTA is not a solution to the problem, it is a method of tackling it.

It can also be a method for avoiding real co-operation, confining the parents' rôle to money raising, denying them any constructive part in the education of their children, and frightening away the inarticulate and timid.

A PTA can be a gimmick. Too often they are the creations of energetic head teachers dragging unconvinced staffs in their wake. In his excellent study of Liverpool schools J. B. Mays makes this point when he writes:

'In addition to much genuine interest and enthusiasm for this aspect of the school's work there has been a good deal of lip service paid to ideas which have either not been translated

[5] H. H. Stern: *Parent Education, an international survey.* Hamburg, University of Hull and UNESCO Institute of Education, 1960, pp. 111-112.

into action or which have been only half-heartedly implement-
ed and at a later date thankfully abandoned.'[6]

Mays points out that a formal organisation, the mere setting
up of a PTA, cannot meet all the needs of the school or of the
parents:

'Other more positive ways of achieving co-operation will
also have to be explored, including the visiting of homes by
either a member of the teaching staff or some other worker
associated with a particular school . . . It is doubtful if, at the
present moment, everything is being done in this direction that
could be done and it seems that for this reason much of the
effectiveness of the educational services within the more
problematic type of neighbourhood is being undermined.'[7]

School reports are sent to most parents. Open days and
evenings are held. How much of this communication is a
one-way traffic—the school telling, exhorting, urging? How
many schools *ask* parents for information? Some ask where
parents can be contacted in case of accident—few ask for
information which would help in teaching children more
effectively. How many report forms ask for parents' comments?

In short, how many schools go out of their way to make
communication a two-way process? How many make it clear
that parents are welcome? How many reflect in their actions
a belief that the parents, through their elected representatives,
own the schools?

On this point Jackson and Marsden express themselves
forcibly and their case is difficult to answer. I believe their
analysis is true of far too many schools. They are talking of
the hurried interviews between parents and teachers on 'Open
Days':

[6] *Education and the Urban Child,* J. B. Mays: Liverpool University
Press, 1962. p. 106.
[7] *op. cit.* p. 118.

21

'Sometimes during these interviews we felt how hopeless the 10 minute annual interview with the teacher was, how stupendously inadequate to the problems emerging. The formal education of the child was continuing, day in, day out, whilst only a few hurried minutes could be snatched to glance at the radical anxieties gnawing at his and the parents' energies.

'What was needed was an utterly different recognition of the parents' place and the parents' rights.'[8]

This chapter started with a description of one parent's first contact with a school. Some work is being done—by teachers and parents—in other schools to improve on that situation. The next chapters describe what was done in one small school; the last chapter of the book tries to sum up the prospects for the future.

In another school in the same city, quite near to the one with the line on the playground, parents had a different reception. There the head teacher asked them to come nearer, welcomed them to the school and said, 'It's nice to see you. We're very busy this morning as you can tell, but if there's anything you want to know please ask. We're always glad to see parents— we want you to feel that this is *your* school.' A few questions followed. The head answered them, then said, 'I expect many of you want to get to work. Before you go I'd like to give you this letter. It says "Welcome" and that's what it means. It tells you the class your child will be in and the teacher's name, the times of our school day and so on. It also asks you to let us know anything about your child which you think may be important. I hope this letter will help you. Please keep it to refer to. You'll notice it says "Please feel free to come and see me if you have any problem about school." Thank you for coming. I hope your children will be very happy with us. And I hope I'll see you all again before long.'

[8] *Education and the Working Class.* p. 207

CHAPTER 2

An Attempt at Improvement

THERE is very little published work in this country relating to parent-teacher co-operation; less still which is the result of practical work by teachers. This chapter is an attempt to improve this state of affairs; it describes a practical experiment carried out a few years ago with the purpose of developing contact of all kinds between the teachers and the parents of a particular school. It is not suggested that the results of this experiment could be applied everywhere. Every school is unique. Nevertheless, certain common factors operate in many schools, and where a group of teachers is convinced of the desirability of strengthening contact with the school's environment, and with the parents of the children they teach, they will no doubt be ready to examine the way in which their problem has been tackled elsewhere.

The school concerned is a small junior school. It is situated in a crowded working-class area in a large industrial city. A large estate of Council flats houses many of the children. Others live in overcrowded older houses which are either condemned as sub-standard or are being gradually cleared.

There are many foreign born children—West Indians, Cypriots, Italians and others—and a floating population, temporarily inhabiting lodging houses and cheap hotels, in the vicinity of the nearby rail termini. There are among the latter many of Scots or Irish descent, and others still from the provinces.

Because of this background there is a fluctuating school population. A 20% turnover of the school roll in a year is not uncommon. In fact, in one period recently from September

23

to March alone, 13% of the children left and their places were taken by others.

The children who live in bad housing conditions bear in their behaviour the imprint of profound and far-reaching problems. Insufficient sleep and privacy, inadequate facilities for washing, for study, simple reading, or recreation and a precocious acquaintance with the seamy side of life; all these have made their mark on the minds of the children before they even attain school age. A survey carried out by the teachers showed that at least a fifth of the children live in conditions of serious overcrowding, in houses without baths or adequate washing and toilet facilities. Even where living accommodation is satisfactory the children concerned have for the most part spent some years in bad housing conditions, and the emotional problems arising in their early years are not automatically solved by rehousing.

The school itself is in an old building. Like so many others it is scheduled for rebuilding, perhaps in the next decade. The most skilful use of its limited resources cannot offset the disadvantages of living in a building erected in the early 1880s. Washing and toilet facilities are inadequate and out of date. Factories and workshops crowd right up to the school's door. One of the city's main roads runs a few yards away. Noise and bustle and dirt and danger are everywhere to be encountered.

There are very many schools like this. But it is not considered that they are the most fruitful field for contact between parents and teachers. Added to all their other problems is that of fluctuation of teaching staff, as many enquiries, such as the Newsom report, have revealed. It is difficult to attract and even more difficult to retain teachers in such areas. During the period under review when the experiment was being carried out there was comparative stability in the teaching staff. But in an earlier period there had been twenty-seven teachers in three years, apart from temporary staff, to six classes.

What kind of teachers took part in the experiment? Most of them were young and keen to put into practice the ideas of modern education. The head teacher, his deputy and one other teacher were older and more experienced, but similarly convinced that it was possible to emphasize a modern approach. The classes were not streamed. Corporal punishment was reduced to the absolute minimum. Competitiveness was avoided and the need for co-operation stressed, while the methods of teaching the basic subjects of English and Number were based on the child developing at his own speed. Class lessons were used to initiate a new section of work, to give direction to projects and schemes, or to sum up what had been achieved, but not to attempt to teach every child on the same level.

Frequent staff meetings and informal discussions were held. It began to emerge that it was not possible to implement modern educational ideas unless the teachers knew a great deal more about the lives of the children and had much more contact with the parents and the neighbourhood. The older teachers were all married and had children of school age, and so they were conscious of the necessity of seeing the parents' point of view and of winning parental understanding and support. It was their firm belief that a great deal of education is wasteful and irrelevant where the teachers either ignore the community or try to insulate the school from it, and where the children as a consequence have double standards of speech, behaviour and moral responsibility.

This point of view is well summed up by H. H. Stern in the report to his survey for the UNESCO Institute of Education, *Parent Education—An International Survey*.

'A clear division of education into distinctly separate provinces of the school and the home is no longer considered possible; schooling to be effective, is regarded as dependent upon the intelligent support of co-operation of parents. Without these, the children are not receptive enough and the

teachers' task is continually frustrated . . . public education
has been found to be ineffective or wasteful if families are
hostile or indifferent."[1]

The suggestions made in this and subsequent chapters are
based largely on the experiment here described. The statistics
and case studies derive entirely from the one school. No
claim is made that they are capable of detailed application
elsewhere. It remains for those engaged in teaching in similar
schools and in similar neighbourhoods to determine what is
of relevance, significance and, possibly, assistance to them.

The methods used to increase home-school contact were as
follows:

a. A new kind of school report
b. Interviews with parents at school
c. Interviews with parents in their homes
d. School functions such as Open Days, exhibitions, concerts, Christmas entertainments, talks by the head teacher
   or inspectors, jumble sales, etc.
e. A parent-teacher association
f. Circular and individual letters to parents
g. Contacts with parents by other means.

Not all these methods originated from the teachers. Once it
was clear to the parents that their help was welcome many
suggestions came from them, and some of the most concrete.
Later chapters of this book discuss these methods in detail;
here it is only necessary to give an outline of how they were
operated.

a. A new kind of school report
The local education authority here, as elsewhere, provides a
printed single-sheet report form. These forms are usually used
as they stand, and rather less widely regarded as inadequate.
They consist of minute spaces in which the class teacher has to

[1] H. H. Stern: *Parent Education—An International Survey*, p. 12.

write significant comment on a child's progress in as many as ten or a dozen subjects, give percentage marks and report on the number of times a child has been late or absent. There is another small space for remarks by the head teacher.

It was decided that the school should design and use its own report, which would begin by telling parents how the child behaved and go on to describe progress as a product of this behaviour. The purpose of the new report form was explained in a covering letter to the parents, which went on to ask for their help.

The first page contained three headings:

'How we see your child at work and play'

'How your child gets on with us and with other children'

'Conclusions and advice'.

Here the class teacher gave observations on the child's reactions at school, in the classroom, the playground, the dining hall and outside the school building. A description was given of the attitudes which seemed to lie behind these re-actions, and of the child's successes and problems.

The second page was headed 'Subject Estimates'. It gave not numerical marks or percentages or class merit lists, but a list of ratings from A to E, with the rating method clearly explained.

The third page was headed 'Parents' Comments'. It asked the parents to give their observations on the report and in addition to write back to the school and give, in confidence, any relevant information about the child's health, interests, problems, history and special difficulties. Finally, this page urged parents to come to the school to discuss their child's progress if they wished.

The reactions of the parents are discussed in the next chapter, but it can be said that this part of the experiment bore immediate fruit. Parents took us at our word and gave us information of the greatest possible value about their children:

'She is an only child and nearly died at birth. I suppose we spoil her.'

27

'His dad died last year and he changed completely.'

'She has three brothers who are all grown up. They take her out and treat her as if she's as old as them.'

'My wife went off and left me last year and I'm sure the twins feel this very much, but they don't like to say.'

'She had eczema at birth and had to be bound for months at a time. It comes back from time to time, but she seems to like school.'

'The lad is very good but both my wife and I are deaf and dumb so it's hard for us to keep him in order.'

In July 1961 reports were sent to the parents of 200 children. 186 parents' pages were returned with signatures. More than two-thirds of those returned made comments, many of them extensive and considered. The comments were studied by the class teacher, passed on to the head and deputy head and analysed into three categories: favourable, neutral, and critical. These three categories refer to the parents' attitudes to the school and its ideas as expressed in their comments. Of 127 comments made, 60 were favourable, 47 neutral and 20 critical, in the main, because parents, of course, often made all three kinds of comment.

The following are examples:

Favourable. 'We would like to thank you and your staff for the tremendous help you have given John during his stay at your school. The patience and encouragement you have all shown has made him a happy and contented boy.'

Neutral. 'I have read his report to him and explained it to him that if he doesn't help himself no one can. He says he will try to do better.'

Critical. 'From different children I have heard that there are favourites in the class and the teacher should try not to show this as it goes against the others.'

Thus the first part of the experiment was quickly proved successful. There was a big response to the idea that parents could play an important part in the work of the school. Many parents commented on the care and hard work put in by the teachers and thanked them for the accurate appraisals made of their children's behaviour. Many parents asked for an interview at the school, and often these were people whom the teachers had never met.

Some of the critical comment was concerned with the disappearance of marks and placings, and with the non-streamed character of the school. Some showed the parents' bewilderment at what they heard about 'modern methods.' Generally, many saw the reports as evidence of the school's desire to make contact, and so the next step in the experiment was to carry forward this work in other ways.

b. Interviews with parents at school

Informal interviews often took place at school as parents came in to see the head teacher with a child returning after an illness, to ask about lost property or for some similar purpose. The parent often took the opportunity to ask about her child's progress, and was encouraged to do so. Other parents would call in to complain about unfair treatment, about bullying or about some misdemeanour. Whenever possible the class teacher concerned would be called in to join the discussion. Parents were never told 'We're too busy to see you.' They were considered to have priority, and if it was impossible to speak to them immediately they were invited to wait and told when the head teacher would be free, or invited to see his deputy, or asked to fix an appointment there and then.

Formal interviews were of two main kinds. Each year parents of the oldest children were interviewed about their wishes for the child's secondary education. After the first issue of the new reports many parents requested an interview, as they were encouraged to do. Often this meant arranging twenty or more interviews in the last few busy days of term, but this was done as far as possible. When it was not possible appointments were arranged for the early days of the following term. And, again, every attempt was made to have the class teacher present at such interviews.

Other kinds of interviews at school concerned children attending child guidance centres. Here the parents were told of the progress of the child, at the centre and at school. Occasionally the parents of a child who was a source of worry would be asked to come for a discussion. Sometimes the behaviour of a child *outside* school would come to the notice of teachers, and it was agreed by the teachers, and by many of the parents, that this was still a proper matter for the school's concern, if not for its jurisdiction. But it is noteworthy that in such a neighbourhood, with one of the biggest areas of organised vice in the world on its doorstep and with all the problems of a colourful but often harsh and violent milieu, that only two children were put on probation in the three years in which detailed records were kept of the effects of parent-teacher contacts.

Many of the meetings at school were too informal to be called interviews. Parents were encouraged to visit the classrooms and meet the class teacher, and many of them did so and showed by their remarks that they appreciated being able to do so. No notice was displayed discouraging parents or warning them that they must see the head teacher first.

c. Interviews with parents at home

Once it had been made clear to the parents that the teachers welcomed the chance to talk to them the need to make contact with parents in their homes arose. Some parents had written to say that while they wished to talk they were unable to come to school because they were both at work all day. It was decided, after consulting the local education authority, to write to all the parents offering them the opportunity to meet the deputy head in their own home, to discuss the progress of their children.

A letter was sent to all the 152 sets of parents, and 48 replies were received agreeing to the visits. The deputy head discussed with the class teacher concerned, before each visit, the history of the child, getting as full as possible a picture of its progress, achievements and difficulties, attitudes and abilities. Copies of previous reports and parents' comments were studied. The Care Committee visitor was also consulted before some visits. A list of questions was prepared and the parents were asked at the beginning of the interview if they had any objection to notes being taken. Some study was made of the technique of interviewing and the interviews were written up and discussed by the staff. Notes of some of these interviews are given in a later chapter, but in order to respect the confidence of the parents, names and certain inessential details have been altered.

These interviews, as well as giving much valuable information, showed the great desire of parents to co-operate and to try to understand what the school was attempting. Some parents made valuable suggestions for increasing the flow of information from school to home and vice versa. For example, two parents made the suggestion that a short report sent after a child had been with a teacher for one term would help to avoid the situation where parents learnt in July that their child was working in such a way with a particular teacher, only to see the child going to another teacher in the next term. Other parents asked for more notice of school holidays and pointed out the difficulties arising when they were in ignorance or when holidays were altered at short notice. Above all, the interviews gave a clearer idea than could be otherwise obtained, of the factors making the children what they were, the pressures they had to contend with and the circumstances directly related to their performance at school. It became apparent to parents that discussion with teachers need not be confined to meetings at school where some of them might feel ill at ease. Moreover, the time involved in a large series of visits convinced even some of the sceptical that the teachers would spare no effort in order to meet them. These visits drew in many fathers who admitted that they tended to leave school matters to their wives; some of them were afterwards seen at school functions for the first time.

The attitude of most of the parents who were visited can be summed up in the words of one of them: 'You certainly leave no stone unturned in trying to see us. There's not a single parent could say you haven't tried to help.'

d. School functions

Full use was made of the many opportunities presented during the school year of inviting the parents to social gatherings. Open Days and Open Weeks were held. Parents of younger children who had recently joined the school were invited early in the first term. In conjunction with the infants' school invitations were sent in July to parents whose children would be leaving to come to the junior school in September, so that both parents and children could see the junior school at work and the transition would be less of an ordeal. Concerts, drama festivals and other events saw parents in the audience. Jumble sales and bazaars were held to raise money. Meetings were organised to explain the modern methods being used in the teaching of mathematics and English. About a quarter of the parents attended such meetings.

At all these functions parents were encouraged to visit the classrooms, see the children's work, and meet the teachers. Many functions were held in the evenings and some on Saturday afternoons, so once again it was apparent that every effort was being made to reach the maximum number of parents. The call on teachers' time was considerable; it was not uncommon to see them talking to parents at 9.30 p.m.

e. The parent-teacher association

A group of parents with children in both the Infant and Junior schools approached the head teachers about setting up, in the first instance, a parents' association. This was done after the circulation of the new report forms, and it was clear evidence that some at least of the parents saw the need for an organised body to canalise support for the school. It was noteworthy, too, that the initiative for this organisation should come from the parents.

The parents' association soon became a parent-teacher association, and began to hold meetings and raise money. Teachers were co-opted on to the committee, and at the first meeting the two head teachers gave a description of a typical day in the life of their school community. Another meeting was held to discuss children's play activities. At these, and at the more social occasions—the jumble sales and bazaars— parents and teachers worked together.

Only a small minority of parents were, of course, actively engaged in the work of the association but it was encouraging to see among them members of the foreign-born communities.

One of the immediate fruits of this venture was the idea that parents should accompany teachers when children were being taken out on educational visits. Another was an invitation to the district inspector to address parents on the new plans for secondary education. On this issue it was clear that many parents were in agreement with the authority's view that the 11 plus selection was becoming outmoded and that a new form of secondary education of a more comprehensive nature was needed.

Apart from this the organisation provided a means whereby the school could obtain a measure of the parents' reactions and this in itself was ample justification for its existence.

f. Letters to parents
Special attention was given to the need to keep parents informed, by letter, of any school activity and the policy adopted by the teachers meant that care was taken to phrase such letters in a friendly way.

c

The practice, so irritating to parents, of giving children information to convey by word of mouth, was discontinued unless there was a very good reason.

Many letters were circulars to all the parents. For example, a change in the school's times in which the dinner 'hour' was lengthened, was conveyed by letter, and the reasons for the change were explained. When parents asked for more information about a report or made critical comment, replies were sent, especially when the parents indicated that they could not come for an interview. The practice of sending letters of praise when children had made noteworthy progress in work or social relations was also adopted. This meant that the receipt of a letter from the school did not invariably produce a troubled reaction.

In these letters to individual parents care was taken to avoid an exhortatory attitude, to enlist the interest and co-operation which would help the child and the school.

When parents came to enter a child at the school they were told something about the way the school worked and given basic information about times, dinners etc. But because it was realised that parents would not remember it all they were also given a 'Welcome letter' which said:

'Dear Mr and Mrs ——

We are very pleased to welcome —— to our school. We hope he or she will be happy with us and find learning interesting and worthwhile. We aim to help every child realise the ability that they have. Our classes are not streamed into As and Bs; they are named after their teacher's initial. As far as we can we deal with the children as individuals. Your child will be in class —— where the teacher is ——'.

The letter went on to give the school's starting and finishing times and other information. It ended with this paragraph: 'We welcome any information you may care to give us, in

34

confidence, about your child's behaviour, health, interests, etc. It there is anything else you may wish to know about our school please do not hesitate to ask'.

g. Contacts with parents by other means

Teachers were encouraged to make informal contacts with parents, and could often be seen talking at the school gate or at the street corner. There was great value in this; mothers, and sometimes fathers, came to know that this was an opportunity they could use to talk over problems which they would not want to put on paper or raise in an interview. One day some parents asked if anything could be done about the thick smoke belching from a factory chimney over their washing —and over the school playground. Action was taken; the head teacher took up this problem with the local council and some success was achieved.

At another time two fathers complained bitterly about the noise and drunken behaviour at a nearby club. Their children were exposed, on their way to school in the morning, to the sight of fights and the sound of foul language as the 'club' clientele emerged into the daylight. Again action was taken, with some success, because the problem was seen as an educational as well as a social one.

Not all the parent-teacher encounters dealt with such wide social issues. More often it was a case of reassuring a mother anxious about a child's progress or talking about a child who had returned to school after an illness, or simply having a chat or a joke.

As relations became more cordial so these 'pavement discussions' became more relaxed and good-humoured. The hard-pressed parents—those who were on the housing list and saw little hope of getting a flat or those on National Assistance—often used this opportunity to tell the teacher their troubles, and it became the accepted thing that any parent could approach the staff in this way.

35

Children were often taken out into the neighbourhood, to sketch and draw, to estimate in the market, to make a census of road or rail traffic, to write a group poem, and for many other reasons. Parents became used to seeing groups of children at the public library or on their way to games in the nearby park, and teachers became used to seeing the environment and the people in it. Often in this situation there was a chance to exchange a few words or to clear up some misunderstanding over a child's absence from school.

Some parents worked at the school, as educational helpers, cleaners or kitchen staff. Hardly ever did they try to use such a position to claim an unfair share of the teacher's time.

All these contacts were used to facilitate co-operation, to show the parents the direction in which the school was working, and to remove misunderstandings and possible causes of grievance.

The way in which individual teachers used these contacts depended on their personalities and experience, but it was clear to the parents that the staff were ready to talk whenever it was possible.

These then were the methods employed by one school to improve relations with parents. The next chapters examine some of the ways in which reports, interviews, school functions and PTAs operate in other schools, and suggestions are made for improvements. There is no doubt that in many schools relations with parents are good and fruitful, and such schools may well be working successfully along the suggested lines. Equally, there is little doubt that there are many schools in which parent-teacher relations could be improved, and, it must be said, some schools in which these relations are poor or even non-existent. But in almost every school there are sure to be teachers who want to know more about the home background and parents who want to know more about school. When a team of teachers work together to improve their knowledge of parents, and try to operate a planned, consistent policy they will be ready to examine what has been attempted elsewhere. But much can come from the efforts of a few teachers and a few parents. In the last situation it is possible to arouse interest among other teachers and parents by using one particular method of developing co-operation. When the two 'sides' come together and results, however modest, are obtained, the search for other methods will naturally arise.

The suggestions made in this book are therefore offered in the belief that there is a vitally important task to be done in appraising the value of ways in which parents and teachers meet and work for the good of children.

CHAPTER 3

School Reports

IN most schools reports are sent out once a year, almost invariably at the end of the school year in July. They are composed for the most part of a list of numerical or percentage marks which are compiled from tests or examinations. The child's overall position in class is usually given, and reference is made to the number of times he has been late or absent. There is usually space for a few words of comment, but not very much. At the bottom of the form there is to be found space for a few sentences from the head teacher.

Infants' schools do not normally send reports. Secondary schools often send more information, but study of large numbers of reports reveals that this information is usually of a statistical rather than a personal nature. Some secondary schools issue cumulative report cards which parents sign and return each year. Some use grades A to E or alpha to epsilon, in an attempt to get away from the odious comparisons of numerical marks. Others, still, use report cards of more than one page, sometimes patterned on various American systems. This type often gives teachers space for more detailed and studied comments. But it seems that secondary school reports are, for the most part, concerned with marks, not persons.

A. W. Rowe, headmaster of David Lister Comprehensive School, Hull, makes this point in an article 'School Reports' in the magazine *Where?* (Summer 1964). He writes, ' . . . most secondary schools content themselves with assessments, however cryptic and fragmented, of the child's academic performance, and give only the barest and most neutral indication of his personal and social growth and development.'

School Reports

The only school report which is favourably commented on in this article is from an army infant school in Cyprus.

Teachers are encouraged to keep careful records of children's behaviour, as distinct from their performance, and many authorities supply record books for this purpose. To do this thoroughly needs a great deal of time. And when it is done it is usually the case that the kind of full comment on a child's confidential record, which is not seen by the parents, is replaced by much terser and more perfunctory remarks on the reports which the parents do see. In most cases the report is kept by the parents; no duplicate is kept by the school.

The writing of reports is yet another task for teachers. It is usually done at the end of the summer term when there are many other calls on the teachers' time—open days, sports days, swimming galas, school journeys, drama festivals etc. In many schools teachers are expected to write reports at home, as well as mark test papers and prepare lessons. This is almost invariably the case in primary schools, where free periods are sparse and irregular if they are found at all.

To criticise school reports is not merely to criticise teachers but to show how they are prevented, by overlarge classes and inadequate facilities and buildings, from doing their job properly. But there is no doubt that in many schools reports are written in a perfunctory manner, and it appears that this is because such schools do not see it as their function to keep parents fully informed. There is certainly no shortage of teachers ready to spend a great deal of their leisure time with their pupils, in many out-of-school pursuits.

What is wrong with the usual school report?

Here are the remarks of some parents when asked this question:

'They don't really tell you anything much.'

'They seem to be telling the parents off, as well as the child.'

'They don't seem to take any account of the difficulties a child has had, like being ill or away for a long time.'

'I don't like the way they always compare one kid with another.'

'They put too much emphasis on competition.'

'You know the child has some real definite worry at school, but the report doesn't say anything about it.'

'If you ask the teacher he tells you one thing, but when you get the report it's a different story. But it's too late to do anything about it then.'

'Well, the report often says something like "He's slow" or "He's not working as well as he should". You know the reason, and often it's not the child's fault, but you don't get any chance to tell the school.'

Many school reports give little real information. They are teacher-centred, full of exhortation—though it is often unclear whether it is the child or the parents who are being exhorted—and written in academic language. They record in a mechanical way what has happened and pay little attention to what could be improved or altered. They are addressed to the parents, but make little or no effort to enlist co-operation. Their manner is often scathing or patronising. They are not really communications but statements. They are out-of-date relics of a past educational era and in no way reflect the new and exciting ideas now being put into practice in many schools.

The typical comments found on reports are stock jokes:

'Trying—very!' or, 'He likes work—he can sit and look at it for hours'. (It should be stressed that I am describing the average school report—no doubt there are exceptions.)

What should a report do? It should give the parents a picture of the child, not just the scholar. It should report on behaviour, not just examination prowess—or the lack of it. It should point out problems with which the child is grappling, problems of health, motivation, social relations, or self-discipline, for example. It should point the way to possible solutions, and it should mention also the successes, however small and seemingly insignificant, the child has had.

As important as what should be done is *how* it should be done. The teacher's use of heavy-handed criticism or sarcasm or academic phraseology usually produces irritation or hostility, and the school suffers because the parents convey their dissatisfaction to the child. If the aim is seen as winning the parents' co-operation, then criticism can be made fairly and carefully, but also frankly. I am not advocating that teachers should adopt the standpoint that parents always know best, or that parents do not sometimes do and say some very foolish things. Children, too, however difficult their circumstances, are at times lazy, bad-mannered, impudent and so on. The real point at issue is, 'How can parents be convinced that they can help the school by understanding what the teachers are trying to do, and how can the behaviour of the children be affected and improved by the greater understanding of their parents?' I have heard a head teacher say to children in the course of a morning assembly, 'Tell your parents not to stand by the school gate and stick their faces through the railings. They look like so many monkeys at the Zoo.' It is quite obvious that in this kind of situation children will adopt two standards of behaviour, one for school and one for home, and come to regard school as a place which has little relevance to life outside.

When there is little contact between home and school, some teachers, it must be admitted, see reports as a means of getting their own back. A teacher who left the school mentioned in the previous chapter wrote to me:

'How useful reports can be in establishing a good relationship between home and school! I find astonishingly few teachers seem to see this as a function of reports. They imagine they are merely a way to reward 'good' children and air grievances about troublesome ones.'

41

What can be done to improve school reports?

1. It would be most helpful first of all for local education authorities to implement, actively, the policies of parent-teacher co-operation to which most of them are, in theory, willing to subscribe. This means among other things that the preparation and writing of reports is seen as a minor piece of social engineering. Schools are given occasional holidays for reasons that are sometimes only vaguely connected with education; why not a regular closure so that teachers could write fuller reports?

2. Again, there are many reasons advanced for having supernumerary teachers in schools, especially those in deprived and difficult neighbourhoods. It would be a profitable use of extra teachers to have them relieve the regular staff, to study records of family history and background, medical records, to write up observations on children, and to do all the other preparatory work which makes reports meaningful.

3. Education authorities which use report forms which have remained unchanged for years could benefit by examining these forms, with the help of teachers and parents. Educational psychologists, training college lecturers and their students could play a valuable part in these discussions.

A useful starting point could be the search for a new name for reports—the word suggests a policeman with his notebook or a drill sergeant. The best kind of report is a record of a child's development in all its aspects. Perhaps 'development record' would express this, but it is also necessary to suggest the child's potential as well as to give an account of his actual performance. Talking about what to call reports should lead to an examination of their function and their underlying philosophy.

4. The single sheet report which is a list of percentage marks and class positions is out of date. It gives teachers no space for considered observations and it stresses competition

by its emphasis on comparing one child with another or by a fictitious and unscientific average.

It is often argued that parents want the competitive kind of report. Little evidence of this was found in the experiment described above. On the contrary, when parents did make comparisons they almost invariably preferred the new style reports. In any case it is part of the teachers' rôle to win the parents for modern ideas, and not to accept tamely prejudices from the past. Because the teachers who argue for competitive reports are not noted for their keenness to communicate with parents in other ways one suspects it is their own prejudices they wish to air rather than the parents'.

5. Educational research has shown how subjective examination marking can be, even at university level. To give an eight or nine-year-old percentage marks for Nature Study, History or English Composition—and this is still widely done —is quite absurd. It would be less absurd if all the teachers of a given school were agreed about standards and if there were less turnover of staff. Of course, any kind of marking or grading implies a comparison between one child and another. Parents are concerned, and quite rightly so, about how their child compares with the average. And here, too, how the grading is explained is as important as what kind of grading is used. Grades must not be presented as eternal verities, categories from which no child can escape, but as tentative descriptions capable of amendment and, above all, of improvement.

6. No report which does not ask for the parents' comments can be considered part of modern education. Not only is it good public relations to invite parents' comments, it gives them the chance to contribute to the school and to the welfare of their own children. It helps parents to identify themselves with the school, which becomes 'we' rather than 'they'. It also gives the teachers a most valuable insight into the thinking of the parents, and into the homes which mould the children they

have to teach. It is, in short, of the greatest value, emotionally, psychologically, and socially.

7.   Methodical reporting should include discussions among the teachers and the keeping of careful records. It is a simple matter to do reports in duplicate so that the school has a copy to refer to. So often a parent comes to a school complaining about a report, and not having brought the actual document with him goes on to quote it from memory. The teacher has no copy but is sure that the quotation is inaccurate, so a long and frustrating argument goes on about what was actually written. If a copy is kept, this situation does not arise.

School copies of reports plus the written comments of parents make a valuable addition to the cumulative records kept on a child; they show, in addition to the child's own development, the attitudes of the parents and, possibly, how the school has helped to amend them.

8.   It is of value also to send some kind of progress report early in the school year, possibly at the end of the first term. Written communication is not a substitute for the careful recording of a teacher's impressions in a permanent form which can be referred to later. Every parent wonders how his child is getting on with the new teacher, and a report sent at the end of the first term would meet this desire for information. It would also reach parents who never come to the school. One term's work would be no basis for a report which emphasized percentages or numerical marks. But one which pointed out a child's difficulties and problems in a constructive way, as well as mentioning the successes and achievements, would enlist the parents as partners in helping the child's development for the rest of the school year.

Such a report would be especially worth while when a child has entered a new school, and a case could be made for a report on these lines to be sent even to the parents of infants.

In the last chapter mention was made of the reaction of

parents to the new kind of report, and some of their comments were given. The new style report was the subject of comment in the national press and on the BBC, and as a result teachers from many parts of the world wrote to the school, asking for copies of the report and showing great interest in the experiment.

Parents' reactions and comments were closely studied and analysed, over a period of two years. Roughly 90% of the parents in this period returned the page which they had to sign. Over five issues of the report an average of 57% made comments. Favourable comments rose from 30% to 49%. Critical or hostile comments fell from 10% to 4%.

Close attention was paid to comments which revealed disagreement with the school's ideas on discipline, which were to reduce punishment, and especially corporal punishment, to the minimum. The proportion of such comments was never very high and fell after each issue of the reports.

The analysis of parents' comments suggests answers to the kind of questions often asked by teachers, especially those who are sceptical of the value of detailed reports. One such question might well be, 'Is there much point in spending hours making careful records of a child's behaviour in order to report to parents? Will parents bother to read the reports, let alone bother to return them?' The answer, admittedly on the basis of one school's experience, is, 'Yes, with careful preparation, nine out of every ten will read what has been reported, and tell the school so.'

To the question, 'Ah, but will more than a handful of parents bother to comment?', the statistics answer, 'Yes, six out of every ten parents will have something to write in reply.'

Another question in the minds of teachers is, 'Will they all plague us with questions about the 11-plus and their children's prospects?' (Or about the G.C.E. if it is a secondary school.) One answer is that if a school makes an examination appear to be of tremendous importance then obviously the parents will tend to attach the same importance to it. The answer given by the statistics in this case was, 'Over a two-year period, out of 953 reactions from parents, the 11-plus examination was mentioned only ten times, i.e., in just over 1% of cases.'

It was found that parents did not try to work off grudges and grumbles, neither were they abusive, except in a very small number of cases; they did not try to interfere with the running of the school, and their comments were not irrelevant, in the main. Of course, parents tried to give reasons for the anti-social and other forms of undesirable conduct of their children. Sometimes they blamed the environment, other children, or parents; sometimes, and with justification, they blamed the tremendous commercial pressures on children; but often they blamed themselves. It was heartening to see parents showing a high degree of self-criticism, admitting their responsibility for some of the undesirable traits displayed by their children.

The analysis shows, too, that children and parents not only were capable of change, but had in fact changed in their attitudes to the school and to education generally. It could be said, in this connection, that a school educates children, but the best schools educate teachers and parents as well.

Parents were rated on a five-point scale when considering their reactions. And the children were rated as making below-average, average or above-average progress.

The diagram on page 48 shows the 953 reactions to reports sent between July 1961 and July 1963. Some parents are represented here as many as five times, others less frequently. I have not given a breakdown of this. There were 111 hostile or indifferent reactions, 250 were non-committal or uncommunicative, 124 were tolerant, 297 co-operative, and 171 very co-operative.

The table on page 49 shows how these categories changed over the two years. It will be seen from this table that hostile comments were not entirely done away with, and that the level of tolerant comments showed little change. Many parents became much more co-operative, but perhaps the most significant change was the reduction in the number of uncommunicative parents.

Examples of reactions are as follows:

a. Indifferent

'I can't help it if she's in trouble all the time— her father was the same before he went off. I learned to let well alone.'

'You say he looks pale and tired. I think they all look the same at this age. Don't think there's much point in taking him to the doctor.'

b. Hostile

'The teachers have always picked on John. They ought not to have favourites.'

'She hasn't learned a single thing. It's not her fault. She's not allowed to get on with her work. There's always somebody putting her off.'

c. Uncommunicative

'Thanks for the report. It's not bad.'

'He's done better this time.'

'I read the report—nothing to say.'

d. Tolerant

'That's her all over. I expect she'll grow out of it.'

'Suppose we can't all be clever. He likes going out to play and I don't want to keep him in.'

'Well, I'm satisfied. I never learned to read much; if he's behind the others he's in front of me.'

e. Co-operative

'We quite agree. We'll take him to the library and see he reads.'

'Sorry about her behaviour—must be very annoying. We've had a little talk with her and she's promised to try. Let's hope so!'

'Thanks to Mr ——, his teacher, he has made progress well. And it shows in better behaviour at home, too. Not so sulky.'

f. Very co-operative

'Certainly we'll come to see you. We are delighted with her improvement, and will do anything you suggest.'

'We are concerned at his poor progress. Would like to meet you and his teacher so we're all working on the same lines to help.'

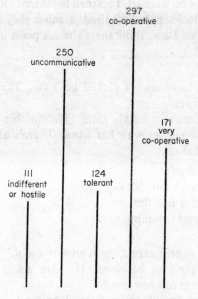

953 Reactions to Reports

'What a grand thing these new reports are! And how well you've arranged them so they really tell us what the kids are like at school. Thanks very much—it must have been a lot of work. There's quite a few things in it that made me think—I'd very much like to come and have a chat but I'll leave it till next term because you must be pretty busy.'

School Reports

CHANGES IN PARENTS' ATTITUDES

	Indifferent or Hostile	Uncom-municative	Tolerant	Co-operative	Very Co-operative
July 1961	32	80	26	47	15
Dec. 1961	22	55	30	60	22
July 1962	20	50	16	69	32
Dec. 1962	20	40	26	61	40
July 1963	17	25	26	60	62
Totals	111	250	124	297	171

To conclude this survey of reports, I am giving examples of the old style and the new, taken from actual reports sent to parents.

OLD-STYLE REPORT

CLASS 2A   NAME Shirley Black   POSITION IN CLASS
24th out of 42

SUBJECT	MARKS	REMARKS
Spelling	40/100	She must do better.
Composition	52/80	Good at times but very careless.
Reading	47/100	Shirley doesn't read enough.
Grammar	38/50	
Arithmetic	27%	Finds it very difficult.
History	35/50	Has done some good work.
Geography	58/80	Good progress.
Nature study	43/100	
Art	52/100	Spoilt by untidiness.
Religious Knowledge	64/80	Good knowledge.
P.E. and Games	40/100	

TIMES ABSENT 5   TIMES LATE 3

49

CLASS TEACHER'S REMARKS

Shirley doesn't do as well as she could. Her marks are quite good at times but she doesn't concentrate enough.

HEAD TEACHER'S REMARKS

Shirley must work faster and set herself higher standards. She behaves herself but wastes a lot of time dreaming.

NEW-STYLE REPORT. Page 1

CLASS M   CLASS TEACHER Miss Matthews
CHILD'S NAME June White   AGE 9 years 4 months

How we see your child at work and play

June is a very quiet child in class. She usually works hard and takes pride in being neat and tidy. She has done some lovely writing and painting, especially in our work on the River Thames project. She is beginning to be more confident in acting and talking—we tell her to try not to worry too much about the other children. In the playground she plays with a few children, but rather hesitantly still, and sometimes she just goes off on her own.

How your child gets on with us and with other children

With adults June is respectful and cheerful. She will talk to us without fear, and quite sensibly. She does not resent correction and in fact the only times she gets agitated are when it is suggested that she should be more patient with other children; She is not confident with other children; she tends to get upset easily. But there are signs that she is overcoming this. We have talked to her about this and feel she is making progress in this direction.

Conclusions and advice

We have tried to give June opportunities to gain confidence in talking to other children, by taking part in plays and in

D2

School Assembly, and in lots of other ways. When she stops thinking, 'They are all laughing at me' she does some thoughtful and delightful work. It might help if you encouraged her to invite children home, if this is possible. Do come and discuss this with us; I am sure it will help June considerably. She tells us a lot about what she does at home!

She has made some good progress and is a reliable, thoughtful child, very considerate of others. Please tell her that she has done well and that we are pleased with her.

I hope you and all the family have a very pleasant holiday.

NEW-STYLE REPORT (Page 2)

SUBJECT ESTIMATES

A=well above average for the class   B=above average
C=average   D=below average   E=well below average

SUBJECT	ESTIMATE	REMARKS
Reading	C	She has tried hard and made good progress. The new glasses have helped. Well done, June!
Speech and Acting	D to C	Clear and sensible speaker, but she is still rather shy.
Original Writing	C to B	Full of interesting ideas. She says what she wants to say quite well.
Handwriting	B	Very neat and stylish—good work.
Music	C to B	A good listener, and a keen singer. Her voice is tuneful and expressive.
Mathematics	D to C	A good trier, but she should not be afraid to ask for help more often—I will not bite her if she does!

Art and Handwork	C to B	June draws well and finishes off her work with care. Now she should be bolder and experiment more.
Social studies (History and Geography)	B to A	Very interested. She has done some fine work, lots of it in her own time. Her improved reading has helped here.
Nature & Science	B	She likes looking after our mice and fish. Very helpful as a flower monitor.
Games and P.E.	D	Still hesitant but she tries to join in.

Class teacher's comment

June has made good progress. She is a real trier and shows real ability and interest in many subjects. She is gaining confidence slowly and appears more relaxed. If we can help her overcome her tenseness I feel we will see outstanding work.

Head teacher's comment

We are pleased at June's progress. We know she finds it hard to speak up and join in, and we feel for her. She has begun to make the effort, with her teacher's help, and has had a little success. I would be glad to discuss this with you and Miss Matthews—early next term perhaps? June has a considerate and helpful nature and contributes a lot to her class. But we feel there is quite a lot of ability in her which we have not been able to help her release yet.

NEW-STYLE REPORT (Page 3)

PARENT'S COMMENTS

(We would be glad if you would both read and discuss our comments on your child, and let us have your own written comments in return. If you would care to write or tell us any information about your child's health, problems and special difficulties, hobbies and interests, this will be of great assistance to us. We will, of course, treat such information in confidence. We have already found information given us to be of considerable value in the way we handle children. If you would rather come to the school and talk about the report, and discuss your child's progress, please get in touch with us and we will arrange a convenient time.)

'Thanks very much for the report—we certainly recognise our June in it! You know she really loves school and doesn't like staying away, even if she's poorly. And what Miss Matthews says is law! We agree she is shy. She's got three older brothers, and my husband says they're too much for her at times, and she wants to get away from them. Mr White was a long-distance driver for years and he used to come in at all hours in those days, so June didn't see much of him—when he was in the house he was usually asleep, and she had to be quiet. Good idea about inviting friends—we'll try it. I'll call in next term and fix to see you. We're grateful for all you've done—our thanks to Miss Matthews. Hope you all have a nice holiday.'

PARENTS' SIGNATURES
Mother. Mary White
Father. J. M. White

CHAPTER 4

Interviews with Parents

'Parents are not allowed beyond this point unless they have an interview with the head teacher.'

The above was seen on a notice in a primary school only three years ago by Brian Jackson, a passionate and persuasive advocate of parent-teacher contact. The school concerned was under the control of an educational authority widely, and justifiably, regarded as enlightened. Clearly a different kind of approach to parents is necessary if fruitful co-operation is desired. After all, the parents are, in the last analysis, those who pay the teachers' salaries and the costs of building, equipment and everything else connected with education. They are also responsible, through their elected representatives, for educational policy and for the running and management of the schools. As individuals they entrust their most treasured possession, their own flesh and blood, to the care of the teachers. While teachers cannot be expected to talk at length to parents at any time of the school day it would help to dispel an enormous amount of frustration if more schools adopted a policy of being accessible to parents.

The usual situation is as follows:

Interviews are almost always held at school, not in the parents' home.

The class teacher is rarely present when a head teacher interviews parents.

Interviews have to be fitted in to an already crowded schedule; they are not an integral part of the school programme; parents usually find that interviews are not easy to obtain.

Few parents try to obtain interviews unless, and until, they have a grievance.

The head teachers who conduct the interviews have had no specific training in the skilled technique of interviewing.

Let us examine each of these factors in turn. In the first place, parents generally do not like going to school for an interview. Many of them feel at a disadvantage; they may have unhappy memories of their own school experiences, and they feel the teachers are more educated than they are. Above all, they do not want to appear to be asking for special consideration for their own child. They feel that the head teacher is the expert. As one parent said to me, 'It's not just having the chance to ask questions. You don't even know what are the right questions to ask.'

For teachers to conduct interviews in parents' homes—and this is done very rarely—most of the staff of a given school must be convinced of the value of such work. They need not all take part in interviewing; this could be left to the head, to his deputy, or to other experienced or interested teachers, though there is no reason why even the most junior teacher should not learn something and have something to offer in visiting parents.

A school could not conduct interviews with some parents and refuse them to others. They would have to be prepared to visit the homes of large numbers and the amount of work involved would be accepted only by convinced teachers. It would help greatly if education authorities provided extra personnel, either teachers or skilled technical assistants. The time is past when we could solve our educational problems by using the voluntary unpaid efforts of the teaching profession, enormous though they have been.

To turn to the second drawback—that when a head teacher interviews parents at school the class teacher is rarely present.

There are few things more infuriating to the conscientious teacher than to be given a résumé of such an interview, suspecting that vital questions concerning the child's reactions in the actual classroom situation have not been dealt with or have been lightly skated over. Even worse, and lamentably this happens much too often, the teacher does not find out about the parent's visit to the school till much later, if at all.

There are obvious difficulties here. If parents are to come freely to the school the class teacher can hardly be summoned from the classroom three or four times a week for half an hour at a time. And, of course, it is part of the head teacher's function to mediate between teachers and parents, and to speak as representative of the school as a whole, of its policy and aims, in a way the class teacher cannot.

At Open Days and evenings it is often possible for parents to meet both head and class teacher, but not in the undisturbed atmosphere vital when a serious difference of opinion needs resolving or a problem has to be tackled. Here, too, it would help considerably if occasional holidays could be used for the purpose of interviews at school. (I hasten to add that I mean *extra* holidays; I am not proposing that teachers should give up even more of their free time!)

In any case, though parents are glad to see the head teacher, it is usually the class teacher—the person who is in close daily contact with their child—with whom they wish to talk.

There are times when a parent comes to school, angry and determined to 'give the teacher a good telling off'. Equally there are teachers who approach interviews in much the same negative spirit. So there is some justification for the head teacher seeing parent and teacher separately, but the main obstacle to fruitful, three-sided discussion is the usual one—lack of teachers. Because if each school could have a supernumerary teacher it would be simple to set aside times for interviews.

This connects with our third point; how to make interviewing an integral part of the school's programme, not an extra burden which means making unsatisfactory arrangements. In the large secondary schools, particularly the comprehensive ones, careers teachers, form masters and mistresses, or house teachers sometimes have sufficient free periods to enable them to see parents regularly. But it is precisely the primary schools where the need is greatest because it is there that the problems often arise, and at a stage when joint action by parent and teacher can more easily lead to effective solutions.

Some schools, especially in the United States, have psychologists, or teachers with psychological training, who deal with behaviour problems by acting as a liaison between school and home. Though it would be an advantage to have such personnel in primary schools the most pressing need is for more trained teachers. If their training included rather more practical psychology than at present, so much the better, but in the primary school at least there is no substitute for contact between the child's parent and his teacher.

It has been said that interviews are not easy to obtain and that parents rarely ask for an interview unless they have a grievance. The two points are connected. It must be admitted that the lengths some schools go to in order that parents should be kept away show an ingenuity worthy of a better cause. One frustrated mother told me she had seen a notice which said, 'The privilege of allowing parents into the playground has had to be withdrawn because some parents have abused it.'

Some authorities do not put the school's telephone number in the directory; I myself have received letters from schools with the telephone number heavily scored out! In other cases head teachers display notices saying they will see parents at such and such a time. This is a big advance but not enough. One such school had a notice saying, 'The headmistress is ready to see parents at 4 o'clock any day.' After some months, when there had been a disappointingly small response, the head asked parents outright, why. The answer was, in effect, 'It would have to be something very serious to bother you with at the end of a tiring day. You teachers have enough to do already.'

In many cases heads would have much more time to see parents if they were given more secretarial help! It is a common criticism of head teachers that they become administrators rather than teachers, and if, in some cases, this is true, it is often because there is not enough help provided to carry out routine but essential administrative and clerical work. For example, if the head teacher has to answer the telephone because he or she has only a part-time secretary, then it is not likely that telephone messages from parents will be so welcome.

Our last point in this connection is that head teachers who conduct interviews have not usually had specific training in interviewing technique. This is not an overwhelming objection. If a teacher has been selected to be in charge of a school he must have had some experience in meeting people, listening to them, distilling the point of view of one group and transmitting it to another. But interviewing is a skilled job. And one has only to witness the lengthy interviews used in the world of commerce to select applicants for quite minor posts to reflect that some of this care could be used in interviewing parents or, for that matter, in selecting teachers.

One large catering firm, for example, uses interviewers with social science degrees or diplomas to give quite lengthy interviews to applicants for such jobs as kitchen porter, dishwasher etc. This is necessary because unbalanced or mentally ill people are an obvious risk to safety or hygiene, and may be working with expensive machinery.

How much more important that those who are engaged in the daily education of children should be selected with the utmost care and skill and should in their turn use similar skill in interviewing parents!

Most head teachers develop the ability to talk to parents by talking to parents. Some do not develop this ability because they simply do not talk to parents. Others talk to parents but do not really listen to what the parents say to them. For example, a parent went to a head teacher to explain that her child's behaviour was affected by a mild form of epilepsy. The head teacher listened for some time and then said, 'Well thank you very much for telling me, Mrs ——, but you must understand we can't put up with naughtiness.'

Of course there are very many head teachers who deal sympathetically and intelligently with parents, making themselves available and welcoming any contact with parents. And there are many others who would be glad to develop further the contacts they have, if only they had the time. Here, too, we come back to the question 'How important is parent-teacher contact?' and the way schools and education authorities answer this question in terms that matter, i.e., in the provision of staff and rooms, for which, of course, they must have money.

WHAT CAN BE LEARNT FROM INTERVIEWS?

Many parents will confide quite important information in the course of an interview, especially if they are convinced that their child's education will benefit, and if they are listened to and treated sympathetically. Some prefer to convey information by letter but there are still many who in their own phrase 'aren't much of a hand at writing'. Teachers who have spent some time at a school begin to know the background of many families. Information trickles in by many routes, some of them devious. Unfortunately mobility among teachers is increasing; the teacher who spends many years at one school is becoming a rarity. There is a need for a more regular, accurate and impartial means of collecting information.

59

Parents and Teachers—Partners or Rivals?

Medical information often gets to the teacher late, when the damage is done. Periodic medical and dental examinations at school are being reduced, and when they are held reveal conditions which have been operating for some time; often they are remedial rather than preventive.

Interviews in the home show teachers immediately the physical background of the child. Interviews at school can convey some of this; whether there is overcrowding, lack of facilities, excessive noise etc. Parents will often say how they are employed and this can be very important. If the father is a shift or night worker it is unlikely that the children should be entirely unaffected. 'Well, her dad does nights, so he won't let her make a noise at all at home. I'm not surprised she shrieks her head off at school,' said one mother. Marital difficulties often come up as an explanation of drastic alterations in a child's behaviour, as parents are loth to commit these troubles to writing. Sometimes the head teacher has to act as a temporary marriage counsellor and this calls for a high degree of skill and understanding.

When parents come to talk about their children they frequently refer to the impact of the neighbourhood. With some it emerges that they dislike their surroundings, feel isolated, and are hoping to move out as quickly as possible. With others there is a feeling of belonging and a corresponding sense of identity with, and pride in, the school.

As well as the information gleaned about the particular child or parents, there are facts about the past history of the school which the teacher can also learn, especially if the parents have lived in the neighbourhood for some years. If not one teacher has been at the school very long—and this is often the case in city schools—it is most valuable to listen to parents who have known the school all their lives and can give an indication of the part it has played in the local community.

In some areas when children leave primary school, head

60

teachers have the duty of evaluating the attitude of the parents towards secondary education—how long they are likely to keep children on, whether there will be financial difficulties, and other related questions. The usual way of doing this is by interviews, but if the parents have not been to the school before it is plainly not so likely that the impressions gained will be as accurate as would be the case where other interviews had taken place in the four years of the junior school, especially if difficulties connected with learning or behaviour had already been successfully dealt with.

A later chapter gives some of the information gleaned from interviews, particularly from home interviews.

It is significant that sixteen groups of parents out of twenty-one who said that their attitude towards the school had changed for the better gave the facility of home interviews as the chief reason for the change, and four groups considered the ease with which they could see the head or class teacher at school to discuss their children to be the main factor. The other nine groups considered the two-way report system the chief factor but seven of these also mentioned home and school interviews as affecting their attitude towards the school.

Finally, on this most important subject of interviews, I would like to quote from a letter by a sincere, perceptive, and very talented teacher, who is also a parent:

'I recall that as a young teacher, some years ago, parent-teacher co-operation was an ideal mentioned at training college but never by my first Headmistress. Teachers never saw parents, except by accident, in the street, because the head ruled that parents should *always* see her first. Open Days were once a year and then just afternoons. Teachers who enquired about a possible PTA were told it wouldn't work in an exclusively working-class area. Any information about children's background came from the Head, who over a long period in the school had built up considerable case-histories

61

and would regale us with some of the more fantastic ones on occasion.

When my own children started school I experienced much of the tension and anxiety that I had never been allowed to see in parents. I was allowed to stay an hour or so on my son's first day—a thing never allowed when I had a reception class— and I saw the whole scene enacted from a parent's point of view. I remembered with horror a child, in my own class, who had spent the first two days weeping at the back of the room, kicking all who approached. Apart from the benefit of a friendly atmosphere, to the child, it has enormous value in helping the mother face a new emotional experience and it reduces the strangeness of the situation for both child and mother.

During my son's Infant school career, and to a great extent his life in the junior school too, I suffered agonies of indecision, about whether to raise various problems with the teacher or Head. I feel that if there had been some time offered—a monthly morning or evening—I should have availed myself of the opportunity. As it turned out, my 'interview' amounted to waiting in a queue on an Open Evening to exchange a few words, terribly conscious of waiting parents and a tired teacher. The main advantage of this exercise was to see his work, and to be able to demonstrate this to him by commenting on certain items. He wanted me to go, I wanted to go but it turned out to be too hurried and superficial to be really helpful. There was no real interchange of information except that I was told his reading age and performance at number.

His Junior School Open Evening was even more disastrous. As a summer-born child with only 2 years in the Infants' School he found a highly competitive system too challenging to face. He was put with children who had had three years in the Infants'. He couldn't cope with mechanical number at their level. All this coming at the transfer to a different school combined to produce a reaction of 'I hate school'. I told the teacher he was unhappy, she replied that he was the only one who was so. She had classified him as anxious and timid during his first half-term but he had now become a naughty boy. She seemed to see no connection between the two states! He was told his position in class—31st—at the age of $7\frac{1}{4}$!

When I raised this point with the Head she agreed it was wrong and said she would rectify it. But the damage was done and his first year in the Junior School was one of misery and frustration. At the second Open Evening at the end of the first school year he was classified as 'unco-operative', 'lacking in concentration', etc. His third Open Day, after 18 months in the school, was more illuminating. He had been given a Group Intelligence Test and was now classified as an 'under-achiever'. At this point I sought the help of the class teacher and Head, but I wonder what would have happened if his I.Q. had been found to be average or under. His problems were fully discussed and investigated and the difference in him as a result was nothing short of miraculous. He has been given extra help to repair gaps and as a result of my being able to fill in the picture of his background and temperament a different approach has been made. He still has problems connected with fitting into a highly competitive system but he is happier and has come to terms with the situation.

Now as a class teacher again in an Infants' School I have come full circle, and apart from the recent publicity given to the subject in the Plowden Report it has been brought home to me forcibly how much good can come from an interchange of information and ideas between parents and teachers.

With large classes it takes time to get to know children individually, and with the best intentions it is easy for a teacher to misread signs or overlook problems. Parents know their children over a long period, have watched their development from one stage to another, have seen certain characteristics disappear with maturity and others persist. Simple information like position in family, relationships with brothers and sisters, emotional attitudes to other children and adults, what facilities there are for noisy play or quiet activities; all these build up a picture of a child and how he sees his world. Children will tell parents what they feel about school, whether they have worries, whether they are happy. All this could take a term or longer for a teacher to observe and valuable time is wasted and the problems may have become entrenched.

Similarly, there are aspects of the child that parents, because of their close contact, may have overlooked or not really appreciated. At my Open Day, run on the same lines as I have experienced as a parent, and therefore unsatisfactory in many ways, with a queue of parents; some of whom told me later that they left after waiting and seeing the futility of the process, nevertheless proved invaluable for certain of the children. How much more valuable would the whole experience have been if the few successes could have been multiplied!

I recall one boy—Johnny—on the surface quite integrated, revealing in his speech a good intelligent approach, but lacking in concentration and seeming more interested in a lark about with the boys than any follow through of a job or activity, even if chosen. Seeing this problem I wondered how to tackle it. Should I isolate him from the boys who seemed to initiate the mischief? Why did he find this kind of behaviour so attractive? According to my assessment of his ability he was very immature in his behaviour; how could I divert his energies to desirable and constructive channels?

I told his parents my dilemma—they supplied the answer. He was an only child, living in a block of flats occupied mainly by retired or business couples, no children nearby, no real facilities for vigorous play, he went home to play with small toys alone. His building with small bricks and arrangements of small model soldiers were left out each night for Daddy to see when he arrived home after Johnny had gone to bed. His parents were aware of the problems and sympathetic about the child's predicament but couldn't do much about it. Johnny was also aware of his lack of progress and this worried him, but it was obvious he wouldn't advance on the learning front until his need for play and contact with other children was well and truly satisfied.

I thought, again with something like horror, what damage I might have done if I had tried to solve the problem without contact with the parents, if they had not come to the school or hadn't been so free with their information. I would have sought some other, probably wrong solution to Johnny's problems. Like my own son he was an under-achiever.'

E

CHAPTER 5

School Functions

THE school year presents many opportunities for inviting parents to social gatherings, from the Harvest Festival in September to the Open Day in July. Many schools invite parents at some time during the year. Yet it is possible for this to happen, indeed for parents to come on several occasions, without any real contact being made. 'Oh of course one has to invite them. Good thing for them to see what we can do with their children. But it's so infuriating when they bring those crying babies'—thus one head teacher expressed herself. And such an attitude is not as untypical as one would wish.

Teachers are naturally anxious that the school should appear at its best on these occasions; should, in fact, demonstrate that it is doing its job well. And it is true that parents will judge the school by what they see and hear.

The work and effort which is involved in the simplest function—a Nativity Play or a talk by a teacher—is considerable. But how often is such work and effort nullified or reduced in effect because no one is deputed to welcome the parents, or because they wander about a three-storey building looking for the right hall or classroom. And so frequently it happens that parents come in, watch a performance, and go out again without a single word being exchanged.

A little imaginative public relations work would be invaluable here. At one school a group of parents wrote the following letter:

'Dear Mr ———,
We the undersigned would like to say how much we enjoyed

66

the plays the other night. Not only that but we really felt welcome. We liked your "welcome to parents" notice. Some of us have been to other schools but there wasn't the same kind of attitude. Once again, many thanks to you and to your teachers for their tremendous hard work for our children.'

The notice referred to was one displayed at the entrance saying:

WELCOME PARENTS!
THIS IS *YOUR* SCHOOL

The plays are being performed in the TOP HALL.

Please feel free to speak to the teachers—
if they aren't surrounded by children!

At the same school notices of a similar character were written in different languages to cater for foreign-born parents. This too evoked a favourable response.

On a wider issue the arrangement of parents' meetings to explain new policies or methods, initiated either by the school or by the education authority, can avoid much controversy and dissatisfaction. P. E. Vernon, in *Secondary School Selection,* mentions the great reduction in complaints over secondary selection in an area where the authority organised parents' gatherings to explain its plans. Similarly where schools begin to implement certain 'modern' educational ideas—reduction or abolition of corporal punishment, 'free writing', projects, and research, which involve children being freed from their desks to investigate the library or measure the playground—some at least of the effect is lost unless the parents are told what is going on and, in some measure, why.

It is interesting to note that at the school under review parents raised problems about their children's health, behaviour and learning, in their comments on reports. In the early stages of the experiment behaviour problems loomed largest but as the teachers gained the confidence of the parents learning problems began to increase in each successive series of comments. For example, while in July 1961 thirty-four comments concerned behaviour and only twenty concerned learning, by July 1963 thirty comments concerned behaviour but fifty-two concerned learning. In discussion and at interviews parents felt free to say that they were confused about 'modern methods', they wanted to help their children but the reply from the child was often, 'But we don't do it like that at school.'

Even with the parents who agreed to have an interview at home—normally an indication of a co-operative attitude - one-third said they did not know enough about what went on in school or that they either had felt puzzled or did not agree with some aspect of modern teaching as exemplified by the school. And a quarter of the parents interviewed at home said they disagreed with the policy of reducing corporal punishment.

For these proportions to admit ignorance or bewilderment at a school, where every attempt was made to explain and to develop co-operation, indicates how widespread confused disagreement may be at schools where it is assumed that parents need not even be told, let alone convinced.

It would appear obvious that on any major change in the school's methods or organisation parents should be informed and, moreover, given a simple explanation.

This is a counsel of perfection. Some schools have no hall, some have one which can accommodate no more than a third of the parents. Some schools are so large that the local cinema has to be hired for Prize Day—hardly conducive to a friendly, intimate atmosphere! But where there is a will methods can be improvised. Classrooms can be used where there are no halls; parents of different years can be seen on separate occasions, as is widespread in the U.S.A. If parents will not, or cannot, come to the school informative letters can be issued like those produced by the old London County Council on

Secondary Transfer or the admirable series produced by
J. E. Mason, late Director of Education at Nottingham, on
such topics as religious education, smoking, sex instruction, etc.

A particular difficulty is that visitors, and especially parents,
like to see a school on a normal working day. But their very
presence often means that it is *not* a normal day. Though it
can be valuable and worth while to talk to parents in the
classroom considerable skill and patience are required for a
teacher to carry on such a conversation while children are
left to their own devices. But still this is done.

At other schools parents are seen in the evening, a method
preferable to many teachers although it is, or should be,
dependent on teachers voluntarily giving hours of extra, unpaid
work after a day's teaching. A compromise is for Open Days
to be held for a week at a time with the head teacher taking
over a class and relieving the class teacher in order that the
latter may speak to parents. Or the children may be split up
and sent to other classes for the afternoon, leaving the teacher
free.

It can be seen, then that school functions offer a great
opportunity for the schools to meet parents, to show what is
being done and what the children are capable of, to explain the
methods being used, and, in particular, where there have been
big changes in such methods. This is generally understood and
widely acted upon.

What is less widely agreed is that parents should not be
the passive audience at such functions, that a school occasion
is, properly, an expression of the joint activity and interest of
teachers, children, and their parents.

In a recent project initiated by the Institute of Community
Studies in London schools, parents were not only visited but
drawn into the daily life of the school—they painted and
mended and sewed, using their several skills in order to
brighten up the school, and at the same time expressing, in a
very practical way, their sense of identity with the school.

Parents will provide money, they will wash the football team's shirts, accompany classes on outings, make tea, and run stalls at jumble sales.

They can also be drawn into *organising* school functions. In fact in many schools where there are successful parent-teacher associations some meetings are left entirely to parents to organise.

As well as chairing or making appeals for money parents can also provide from their number interesting speakers on topics related to education. Not only doctors, dentists and actors but also shopkeepers, trade unionists, and others can contribute much which is relevant to the work of a school.

CHAPTER 6

Informal Contacts

'IT WAS a source of nourishment to me to be on friendly terms with pupils I was teaching and to be able to talk to them and their parents in shops and on the streets. It didn't matter what class they came from.[1]

In the idyllic village described by 'Miss Read', the teacher is a focal point in local life, at least for those who have children at her school. And no doubt there are some schools where reality is not very far removed from the picture she paints, with the teacher, as a social figure, poised somewhere between the vicar and the policeman. Where the teacher lives in the school neighbourhood, and is a part of it as an individual, to contact parents outside school is relatively simple.

The position in urban schools is very different. Mention has already been made of the increased mobility of the teaching profession, relative to 1939. The inclusion some years ago in the salary structure of special allowances gave a further incentive to young teachers to move. In a large city teachers tend to live in 'middle-class' areas when they have been teaching for more than a few years and have escaped from the poky but expensive bed-sitters which is all they can afford at first. Schools in working-class areas tend to be staffed by teachers who live miles away and, what is perhaps worse, regard themselves as having little in common with the social mores of the area where they work.

[1] Harry Rée, formerly headmaster of Watford Grammar School, and now Professor of Education at the University of York, in an article 'The Man who changed his mind.' *Where*, Spring, 1965.

It is possible to promote informal contacts in such areas, but only if the teachers cease to see the school as 'an island of culture surrounded by a sea of barbarism'. Modern education sees a school as 'a base not a barracks'. Many teachers who begin by being not very sympathetic to the idea of contact with parents will nevertheless explore the least promising of neighbourhoods to stimulate their children to talk and paint and study for projects.

'Local studies' are the most realistic way of awakening the child to an awareness that history and geography and science and nature study are not merely 'subjects' to be learnt within the four walls of the classroom but different, related ways of looking at the neighbourhood in which he lives. The young teacher is sometimes surprised to find that the neighbourhood, as well as having canals, docks, street markets and level crossings, has people.

Talks with mothers who stand at the school gate are the first contact most teachers have with the parents of the children they teach. It is always interesting to stop and exchange a few words and a joke. In this kind of friendly atmosphere parents will say things and reveal problems which they would hesitate to write down; problems of overcrowding or discord at home, explanations of a child's absence from school, queries about a message from school which has been received in a garbled form, and so on. If teachers are encouraged to stop and talk for a few minutes what they say is not so important as the impression they are giving of being friendly and interested participants in the lives of others.

Mothers will often display their latest baby, or introduce a toddler who will be coming to school soon. At times they will be accompanied by an older child, who has left the school, and will give an account of his or her progress at secondary school. In these surroundings teachers can realise the importance of the school and the part it plays in the continuing life of the community.

Yet here, too, the ingenuity of some teachers in their determination to avoid contact with parents is worthy of a better cause. Schools have been known to instruct teachers not to bring children in from the playground until parents have departed, to restrict parents to waiting at one gate while teachers enter by another. Indeed, I was specifically told by one head teacher not to spend so much time talking to parents at the gate 'because other parents will think you are giving their children preferential treatment'.

On one occasion I was approached by a group of mothers outside school and asked if I would take up with the police the question of parking in the narrow and congested street in which the school stood. On another occasion when a teachers' salary dispute was in the news a mother asked if she could organise a petition in support of the teachers' claim. It was most heartening to hear the expressions of support coming from all sides, and to see this support being given very practical expression as parents queued to sign a letter to their MP. (It was noteworthy that the organiser was a mother who had previously visited the school to complain about her daughter being unfairly treated.)

Parents will also be encountered when children are being taken to the local library, the park, or the railway station for a more distant excursion. Where a school encourages teachers to take children out of the classroom and into the surrounding streets these encounters will be more frequent and it becomes quite natural for a teacher to stop for a few minutes to chat.

Some schools are physically isolated from the neighbourhood, behind high walls or in the middle of fields. Where this is so it is necessary to make efforts to counteract isolation. Teachers should be encouraged to explore the neighbourhood, to eat in the local restaurants, to borrow from the library, and to visit the local park. Students visiting schools for teaching practice or observation could well be taken on a tour, taking in the Council flats, the community centre and library, and also to see the launderette, the secondhand clothes shops, pubs, sweet shops and cinemas which the children have seen and been influenced by since they were first pushed past them in a pram.

Parents frequently work in the school and this enables informal contacts to be made quite simply. Schoolkeepers, kitchen workers, welfare helpers and cleaners all have children. In a school where parents are valued, treated, that is, as equals and not as potential disturbers of the peace or askers of disturbing or impermissible questions, a great deal can be learnt about the neighbourhood—and about the school itself. In some schools the welfare or educational helpers, usually local mothers, make a contribution out of all proportion to the wage they receive—providing a stable mother figure, doing first-aid, making tea, and acting as a link between the school and the home. Where teachers come and go these women are centres of stability, and, as well, an unrivalled source of can help in forming all kinds of informal contacts with the knowledge, social and geographical, about the neighbourhood. They identify themselves with the school and many are as ready to sacrifice spare time as the teachers. Used wisely they world outside, particularly because of the tact they have learnt, as parents in a teachers' world. (One such mother helper, on being told by a young teacher that the children of the locality were 'scruffy and bad-mannered', replied, 'Well, Miss X, that'll all change when you've been here a few years').

Not all teachers have the experience or the desire to use these informal contacts to the full. It is the responsibility of the Head and other experienced teachers to show that contacts can be made without favouring one parent more than another, without the teacher losing dignity or ultimate responsibility for the organisation of the school or the classroom.

CHAPTER 7

Case Studies (I)

EFFECT OF PARENT-TEACHER CO-OPERATION ON THE CHILD

PARENT-TEACHER co-operation brings many benefits. It identifies the parent with the school, helps the teacher to understand the neighbourhood, and reduces conflict and tension on both sides. Moreover, it begins to make the democratic control of education a reality at what the Americans would call the 'grass roots' level.

But all these advantages are incidental; the educational reason for parent-teacher co-operation is that it helps children to learn better. By acquainting the teacher with the child's background, the factors which make for stress and tension as well as those which produce stability, and by passing on to the parents the relevant facts about the child's attitudes and behaviour at school, it is claimed that the child's school life becomes more meaningful. Life is no longer divided into two categories, 'home' and 'school', in one of which you relax and enjoy yourself while in the other you 'learn'. Children no longer feel their parents and their teachers exerting different kinds of pressures on them for different, conflicting aims.

The following case studies show what happened to children whose parents became more co-operative. Their initial attitude towards the school was hostile, or at least very critical. The selection has been made at random. (The names and other inessential details are fictitious.)

1. BOY: ROBIN

Parents' reactions to report in July 1961. Form returned without comment though Robin had been in constant trouble and was below average. Father came to school and said boy was being unfairly treated, had an angry interview with class teacher. Next term Robin ran home twice, swore at teacher and was a constant source of trouble.

December 1961. Form returned with laconic comment 'A very bad report'. Parents ignored invitation to interview.

July 1962. Report returned without comment though it again stressed that the boy's attitude could be changed with co-operation from home.

December 1962. Robin now in his last year. Conduct so bad he was moved from fourth- to third-year class to be with deputy head. Parents agreed to home interview and in fact two long interviews took place in the parents' flat. Parents replied to December report quite fully and in a helpful way, and began to call occasionally at school where friendly talks took place.

July 1963. Robin had had occasional bouts of defiance but was generally much improved. Final report pointed out again his many good qualities and mentioned some which had only just appeared, attributing these to the stability arising from contact between school and home. It also mentioned behaviour tendencies which, if not corrected, could lead to trouble in the secondary school.

Parents commented, 'We wish to thank the headmaster and all the teachers for helping Robin.'

In this case the child's performance improved from well below average to average; the parents' attitude improved from markedly hostile to reasonably co-operative.

2. GIRL: JANE

July 1961. Jane finished her third year in July 1961. She had been in the class of a young teacher in her first year out of training college. The teacher agreed that she found it difficult to appreciate the problems of the community and found the

76

children exhausted her. Jane had not got on well with her teacher who found her a quarrelsome child. Her progress was described as below average, scholastically and socially. The mother returned the report form with extended angry comments. She complained that the child was being unfairly treated and 'picked on'.

December 1961. Jane, now in her last school year, had moved to a more experienced teacher, who established friendly relations with the mother, at first by talking to her at the school gate. This developed into an invitation to come to the classroom and see the child at work.

Jane began to make progress approaching the average in her work; socially she was much stabler. It emerged from conversations with the mother that Jane was jealous of an older brother. Both parents signed the report form and said they were encouraged to see some improvement.

July 1962. Informal conversations with the mother continued. Father had also visited the school and expressed his pleasure. Jane appeared more settled and was much more communicative. Outbursts of temper became rare, and her range of interests and friendships widened. Her work maintained a better level, in some subjects being above average.

Parents commented on the last report, 'This report shows a great improvement in Jane during 1962. We are very glad and send our thanks to you all for helping'.

The dominant parent, the mother, moved rather rapidly from a hostile position to a very co-operative one. The child made some academic progress, from below average to average, and, in some subjects, a little above.

Socially, her progress was rather more significant.

3. BOY: CHARLIE

July 1961. A boy with a very dour manner, big for his age, with certain qualities of leadership. His speech to teachers

77

was confused and shy and very Cockney. His work was significantly below average for the class and clearly below what he was capable of. His main energies in the school were spent in leading a group of boys in petty excursions against authority. The report put these points and described the boy's progress as below average. Parents ignored the report.

December 1961. Charlie's work and conduct continued to decline, and his escapades became more serious. One concerned an attempt to flood the school by turning on all the taps in the cloakroom. He seemed to try to dominate all the children he came into contact with and to be afraid of teachers. His report made these points but again it was ignored.

July 1962. There had been some considerable improvement— a fortnight's school journey had taken place just before Easter and Charles was persuaded to go. Here he had the adventurous open-air environment he needed and was able to release his energies without continual conflict with authority. He found, too, that the other children on the journey were not so ready to follow him unless what he proposed was acceptable. His mother was very pleased with the result, and came to the school to say so. His work began to improve and to approach the average. In a school musical play he emerged as an actor of humour and skill and his parents coming to the performance, commented, 'Well, you've got him going on something useful at last—we're very pleased.' His report, the last in the junior school, described the improvement and stressed that it couldn't have taken place without some co-operation from the parents. The parents returned the form and made extensive co-operative comments.

In this case the school's readiness to take the boy on a school journey despite his tendencies to act against authority convinced the mother of its good intentions. Both parents moved from a hostile attitude to a reasonably co-operative one. The boy's work moved from below average to average and in some subjects—games, drama, art—to above average. His behaviour was radically improved; persistent anti-social and destructive tendencies were channelled into constructive fields with only minor lapses.

4. GIRL: SHEILA

July 1961. Sheila's report described her work as a good average but her conduct as 'unco-operative and sly'. The father ignored the report; the mother signed it but did not comment, and both ignored an invitation to come and talk.

December 1961. By this time Sheila had been in another class, in her second year, for four months. The class teacher was young and inexperienced and found her difficult to control. Her report described her as working below ability and very quarrelsome. The parents replied with lengthy comment blaming the teacher for 'having no patience with Sheila', but they said they would come and talk it over and did so, giving a lot of information, in particular on her relations with her older sister who tended to dominate her. Still, relations with the class teacher continued to be unsatisfactory. On one occasion the child's grandmother accosted the teacher in the street and tried to argue.

July 1962. Sheila's report spoke of a small improvement and occasional bursts of defiance. Sheila had made a little progress, but there was no reply from her parents.

December 1962. Sheila had been with a more experienced teacher this term. Also, the teacher had met both parents at the school gate and had begun to talk to them. Their response was friendly but still guarded, until a few months after Christmas, when they asked the teacher to come and see them at home.

At the home interview a great deal was learnt. The family's accommodation was shocking—two basement rooms in a dark and noisy house for two adults and four children. The parents said they felt the school did not realise their difficulties, but they were appreciative of the fact that we wanted to find out, and to help.

July 1963. Sheila had made a great improvement. She went on the school journey, became a keen swimmer, and became much more relaxed with children and adults. Both parents became regular visitors to the school, and the report spoke of all-round improvement. Parents' comments were full and enthusiastic.

December 1963. Family left the neighbourhood. Sheila's report spoke of her continuing to make well above average progress, and becoming very popular with other children. Her parents wrote to the school thanking the teachers and saying 'We're sorry we were so suspicious about the school. You've done wonders. We'd like her to stay with you but it's much too far for her to travel.'

May 1964. Sheila's parents wrote to say Sheila had been accepted at a grammar school—'Thanks to you, we know.'

5. BOY: KEITH

July 1961. Keith was the oldest of a family of four children who had recently come to the school from Wales. He was very talented in music and art, but his work in the basic subjects was slapdash and well below his apparent ability. Uncertainty in a strange environment caused him to assert himself in anti-social ways—exaggeration, lies, bullying, etc.

His mother was often away from home and Keith was kept from school to look after young children. His hearing was poor but he often refused to wear his aid.

His report put these points in a constructive way, but it was returned without comment, signed by his father only.

December 1961. Keith's conduct improved slightly as he began to find his level with other children. But his work was still poor and below what was felt to be his capability. His report was again signed only by his father and without comment.

But he signified his willingness to come to school to discuss Keith with the class and head teacher.

The interview took place in January 1962. Both parents were present. The mother began in a very aggressive way until the husband suggested she go outside to 'cool down'. She did so and he apologised and began to discuss things in a rational way. The wife reappeared, apologised, and joined in. Resulting discussion was fruitful, acquainting us with several important facts.

July 1962. Significant progress was made in these six months. Keith was absent only rarely and wore his hearing aid—two points his mother had promised to attend to. The improvement in his work was accelerated; in English it came up to average, in mathematics and most other subjects it was significantly above average. Socially, he remain argumentative and pugnacious but these tendencies were less marked.

He left the school in July 1962 and his last report was an excellent one. His parents commented extensively on the return sheet. Their more co-operative attitude was maintained in the next few years with the two younger sisters.

6. GIRL: JANICE

July 1961. Janice was in her third year at this time— a very quiet and excessively timid child, so far below average as to be at or near the sub-normal level. Her report described her as well below average in attainment and as withdrawn and troubled. Her parents replied, vehemently disagreeing and saying that the teacher's observations were worthless. They refused to discuss the matter further.

December 1961. Janice remained basically the same in her next class and a similar report was sent, suggesting that the school could help. The report was returned, again disagreeing but mentioning some of the problems the child had.

The family lived in a squalid area and they said Janice was terrified by the noise of drunken rowdies at night. She was in

F

poor general health, slept badly and had nightmares.

A sympathetic letter was sent from the school suggesting action the parents might take to improve matters, by approaching the police etc. The parents replied in a co-operative way but would not come to the school.

July 1962. At this stage Janice left for a secondary school. Her report said she had made no real progress but pointed out ways in which she could be helped at her new school. Her parents returned a short and rather non-committal comment.

In this case no real advance was made with the child, and only a little with the parents.

These case studies show that changes in children were connected with changed attitudes in their parents. From the cases of children studied over three years it emerged that one child out of two with co-operative parents made above-average progress; only one child in four with unco-operative parents made above-average progress. Children of parents who were initially hostile stood much more chance of making progress if their parents became co-operative than if they remained hostile. The following diagram shows what happened with seventy-eight children whose parents' initial reaction to the school was one of hostility:

PROGRESS OF CHILDREN OF INITIALLY HOSTILE PARENTS

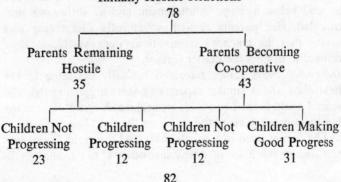

Initially Hostile Reactions
78

Parents Remaining Hostile
35

Parents Becoming Co-operative
43

Children Not Progressing 23

Children Progressing 12

Children Not Progressing 12

Children Making Good Progress 31

F2

Case Studies (1)

But as well as showing how children began to progress as their parents moved from hostility to co-operation our investigation showed a definite, statistically significant link between co-operative parents and children making progress which was average or above, as the following table demonstrates:

EFFECTS OF PARENTS' ATTITUDES ON CHILD'S DEVELOPMENT

Attitudes of parents	Child's progress	1961	1962	1963
Co-operative	Average or above	36	54	70
	Below average	39	55	65
Unco-operative	Average or above	32	28	17
	Below average	93	50	38

Not every improvement in parents' attitude led to a better performance from the child, and it was often observed that behaviour improved while a child's work performance remained fairly constant or took much longer to improve.

There was general agreement among teachers that it was much easier to deal with the children of co-operative parents. But there were exceptions to this, too; some children with great behaviour problems had parents who were most co-operative, because the very gravity of their child's difficulties caused them to seek help from the school.

The knowledge that their parents were in constant, friendly contact with their teachers was a steadying influence on many children and, in particular, on the two age extremes—the oldest children, on the verge of adolescence, and the youngest, who had only recently come from the infants' school.

This kind of co-operation can only be achieved by constant effort, and even after hard and unremitting activity by the teachers there was still a hard core of parents who ignored every overture. But in the conviction that, just as almost every child is capable of improvement so almost every parent can be won for co-operation, many teachers persist in trying to develop contacts in the knowledge that the child will ultimately benefit. It is hoped that this chapter will, in small measure, serve to reassure and sustain such teachers.

CHAPTER 8

Case Studies (II)

RECORDING HOME INTERVIEWS

'THERE has got to be a greater sense of pastoral care for the individual boy or girl who goes to school. You have got to know them as individuals, visit them in their homes, and know their background before you can find the art and skill of teaching them.'[1]

The previous chapter traces the effects on the child of the changing attitudes of the parents as they became more co-operative towards the school. Parents who agreed to have an interview in their homes were, of course, more co-operative than the average, and this chapter contains a selection of these interviews. These home interviews are rare, and in view of the light they shed on the process of communication it is felt that they are worth presenting here.

In selecting, care has been taken to make the sample given representative. The notes deal with parents whose difficulties were significantly affecting the school lives of their children, or with those who were especially co-operative. So it is possible to see the gravity of some of the factors impinging on a child, and, in an optimistic way, to see that the very gravity of these problems makes some parents respond readily to help when it is offered.

The names, occupations and locations given are fictitious. Irrelevant details have been altered and sometimes excised. This has been done because the information given in the interviews was confidential.

[1] From an address given to training college students by J. E. Mason, late Director of Education, Nottinghamshire, January 20, 1963.

Parents and Teachers—Partners or Rivals?

1. VISIT TO MR & MRS JONES

(i) *General impression of home and parents*

Mrs Jones is well known to the teachers as she brings the children to school every day. She is a cheerful woman, always ready for a joke. Mr Jones has been to the school, to parents' gatherings, but not often as he works long hours in a restaurant.

They have five children, all boys, ranging in age from two to ten years. They live in two rooms and have to go down to a landing for water. The street is a very busy main road where traffic noise hardly ever ceases.

Despite their terribly inadequate housing Mr and Mrs Jones are good-natured and tolerant, keen for their boys to learn and anxious to co-operate.

(ii) *Main points covered in interview*

Interview took place from 7.30 to 9.15 p.m.

a. Both parents said they felt welcome at school and able to talk about their problems. They said they were grateful that the head teacher had written to the Council backing their plea for better housing.

b. They both mentioned the new report form and said they had found it helpful and the comments on it true.

c. They said they felt they knew all they needed to about what goes on in school. Mrs Jones said, 'Well, your school goes out of its way to tell parents. Most schools don't.'

d. They were not perturbed about modern methods of teaching but were glad to hear more about it from me.

e. On discipline they thought teachers should be allowed to smack or cane. They both said they didn't like smacking and felt upset when they did it, generally as Mr Jones said, 'When things get on top of you and the kids don't understand.'

f. They felt that the school gave their boys 'as good a chance and as sound an education as you'd get anywhere'.

(iii)   *Information learnt*

That the family is Catholic. That Mr Jones is in the catering trade. That the boys are possibly left-handed—this is being investigated. That the oldest boy, Dick, is sensitive about undressing for games, because, as Mrs Jones said, 'His clothes aren't always of the best.'

(iv)   *Problems discovered*

No new problems except as above. The children are very quiet, pale and sometimes tired looking, with bursts of temper or tears.

(v)   *Parents' attitudes to school and education*

They were keen for their children to benefit. Mr Jones spoke of being unemployed for a long period because, he thought, he had been to a church school which 'wasn't interested in education; only in religion'. Both parents spoke rather disparagingly of other schools where the teachers had, they felt, been curt and unwelcoming.

(vi)   *Summing-up*

Though Mr and Mrs Jones have always been friendly and co-operative the visit was very useful. It emerged in discussion that a teacher had spoken sharply to one of the boys, saying he was too tired to work because he watched too much television. The parents had resented this; they did not, in fact, have television. They felt the teacher did not appreciate how difficult it was for them to get five children to sleep in two rooms, one of which they were using themselves. Because of this they had refrained from comment on the report form. They agreed that it would help teachers if they did comment and said they would do so in future. Subsequent reports were returned with informative comments from the parents.

2.   VISIT TO MRS SULLIVAN

(i) *General impression of home and parents*

Mr Sullivan was at work. Mrs Sullivan was a young Irish woman with six children, the oldest a boy of thirteen, the youngest a baby of four months. She told me she was twenty-nine. Their living accommodation was shockingly inadequate —two basement rooms, small, damp and ill-lit. The husband was a labourer. The couple had previously been to the school and it had emerged that the wife had contemplated leaving her husband. She suffered from nervous trouble.

Despite all her troubles she was cheerful and hospitable, and spoke warmly of the help she had received from the school and from the Care Committee. She had three children in the Junior school, Mary, an excessively quiet and nervous child of eleven, Brendan, who is nine and much more extrovert, and Michael, a cheerful and placid seven-year-old.

(ii) *Main points covered in interview*

a. Mrs Sullivan was quite open about the difficulties with her husband. 'He won't mind me talking about it. We're getting on a bit better now, but it helps to talk to somebody.'

She said it was impossible to hide these troubles from the children, especially the older ones, and this must affect them and their performance at school.

She said she always felt welcome at school but did not like to go too often—'It seems I'm always asking you for something.' I said we were only too glad to be able to help and that she mustn't feel diffident.

b. She welcomed the new report form and had persuaded her husband to write down his comments on it.

c. She said she felt she knew what the school was trying to do, but her husband did not agree with its aims.

d. She did not really understand modern methods of education, but had had more than enough experience of formal methods

88

in her own schooling in Dublin. The local priest had visited her and urged that the children be sent to a Catholic school. Her husband agreed with the priest but she had refused, saying 'They get their religious instruction at Church. Besides I can tell that at your school they really care about kids. I don't want them to go anywhere else. They love school and they're forever telling me things they do.' I pointed out that she could have the children excluded from Daily Assembly to counter any religious objections.

e. On discipline she said she was used to corporal punishment at her own school, and found it difficult to control her children without it—or even with it! But she agreed that it often aggravated children's problems. Here again her husband disagreed!

(iii) *Information learnt*

That Mary has been complaining of headaches and would do well to have another eye test. That she is worried because she has begun to menstruate.

That Brendan, despite his age (nine) has very decided views, imbibed from his father, about the female sex and its inferiority to the male!

Other information as in para (i).

(iv) *Problems discovered*

That Michael has some kind of speech defect. That Mr Sullivan is away from home for long periods, working overtime, and that he is at loggerheads with his wife on many issues concerning the upbringing of children.

(v) *Parents' attitudes to school and education*

Mrs Sullivan was ready to co-operate with the school as far as she could, despite her differences with her husband. Her attitude was simple; the school was able to help her and she needed all the help she could get. It was necessary to make clear that the school could pass no opinion on the religious questions on which the parents differed, and this Mrs Sullivan accepted.

(iv) *Summing-up*

The interview was not very long—about one and a half hours. With the husband not present it was not possible to go into questions of discipline and modern education at great length. Still, it was valuable to see at first hand the great difficulties the family had, and Mrs Sullivan appreciated this.

3. VISIT TO MR & MRS MATTHEWS

(i) *General impression of home and parents*

Mrs Matthews had been to the school quite often; Mr Matthews never. They had one girl, Teresa, ten, at the school, and a younger boy, aged four. Mr Matthews was a carpenter. Mrs Matthews said at the beginning that she was a very religious woman but did not mention her denomination. She said her beliefs influenced all her actions; she had had a nervous breakdown seven years earlier and this had affected the girl very much. Teresa was a self-possessed, rather grave child, above average in intelligence but looked pale and not robust.

(ii) *Main points covered*

a. Mr Matthews said that he did not share his wife's religious views, but they had both agreed to take Teresa away from a church school because they objected to its emphasis on competitiveness and lack of communication with parents.

There was some disagreement between the parents about the extent of Teresa's problems. Mrs Matthews attributed the child's withdrawn nature to the nervous illness she herself had suffered. Her husband, on the other hand, thought Teresa resented her younger brother.

Another source of conflict admitted by the parents was that

Mrs Matthews disliked the neighbourhood and called it 'immoral and sinful' while her husband liked it and resisted the idea of moving out.

b. They agreed that the new report form was a good innovation. They welcomed its emphasis on co-operation rather than competition.

c. They said they agreed with what they knew about modern education, but criticised themselves for not coming more often to the school. Mrs Matthews doubted whether the neighbourhood was the best place to try out modern ideas.

d. On discipline Mr Matthews thought corporal punishment wrong; his wife thought it appropriate for some children but not for others.

e. Mr Matthews was keen for Teresa to stay at the school, saying 'We moved her from that church school because they were only interested in the bright kids. When we spoke about her problems they weren't interested.' Mrs Matthews said, 'Perhaps it's me; if I felt I could settle down here I wouldn't want to uproot the family, I've no quarrel with the school but you must admit it's a tough place to live.' She mentioned that Teresa had to pass a street on her way to school in which there were two brothels. Fights and unsavoury scenes were a regular occurrence. She asked me, 'Would you live here? You've got young children.'

I said I would, but I shared her apprehension. I pointed out the good features in the community; the presence of many people and organisations working to improve and clean up the district.

Mr Matthews said his wife was really not a good mixer; the character of the area was an excuse. His wife replied that he 'may be half-right'.

(iii) *Information learnt*

The nature and extent of Mrs Matthews' dislike of the

neighbourhood. The possibility that Teresa resented her brother.

(iv) *Problems discovered*

The conflict between the parents on whether or not to move and their respective assessments of the value of the school.

The problem of Mrs Matthews' self-isolation. Her husband said 'she feels she could go out to work—we could certainly do with the money. But she won't because this would be making roots here.'

(v) *Parents' attitudes to school and education*

Both parents spoke with some understanding and insight about education. They understood what the school was trying to do. Mr Matthews in particular praised the new report form: 'That's a damn good idea. It really shows how a child works—not just how many marks she's got.'

(vi) *Summing-up*

This was a very useful interview because it conveyed the conflict felt by some parents between dislike of the noise and violence of the neighbourhood and appreciation of the aims and work of the school.

4.　　　　VISIT TO MR & MRS SAKUNTLA

(i) *General impression of home and parents*

Mr and Mrs Sakuntla are Pakistanis and their religion is Mohammedan. They have four children, three girls and a boy, all of them in our school. They live in three rooms in a very old house and are paying an extortionate rent.

The father is a clerk and speaks English well; the mother's English is much more halting.

Mr Sakuntla has been in England since shortly after the last war, in which he fought in Burma, attached to a British regiment. His wife has been in England for ten years. They both felt that English schools were very superior to what they knew in Pakistan. There, they said, most of the schools were religious ones and their methods were formal and antiquated.

(ii) *Main points covered in interview*

a. Mr Sakuntla was very enthusiastic about modern education. He was interested when his children had told him about a United Nations Day service at the school when the idea of racial tolerance had been developed.

b. Both parents were keenly concerned about the effects of racial prejudice and listened carefully when I told them what the school was doing to combat it.

c. Mr Sakuntla was surprised to learn from me that the new report form was not universal. He had taken copies of it to work and it had been discussed there, but his colleagues had not mentioned the kind of reports their children received. He said, 'I can see we'll have to have another discussion.'

d. On discipline the father said he was against corporal punishment but his wife said she thought English mothers gave in too much to children.

e. They both thought the main problem with their children was the lack of contact they had with English children outside school. The oldest girl was ten and she had many friends, some of whom came to the house to play. I said this was a good idea and that it would help if the children were allowed to join local clubs, go to the library etc.

(iii) *Information learnt*

That the youngest girl, aged seven, had a speech defect which had not previously been reported.

That the little boy, Raji, had kidney trouble and difficulty in controlling his bladder. I said I would tell the teacher concerned.

That Mrs Sakuntla would soon be going out to work. ('I don't want to but we need the money badly.')

(iv) *Problems discovered*

Mrs Sakuntla could not speak much English and was rather dreading going out to work because of this. I sympathised and said it would be a great help to her, and especially to the children, if her English were more fluent.

She was worried about the effects of racial prejudice, and so was her husband, but to a lesser extent. I said that I was utterly opposed to such prejudice and that the school, which had Irish, Greek, Italian, Indian, Pakistani and other pupils, worked hard to make integration a reality. Mr Sakuntla was delighted to hear that I had fought in Burma, too, and said to his wife, 'You see, we fought for these things in the war—now we still fight together.'

(v) *Parents' attitudes to school and education*

Mr Sakuntla much admired our school and English education in general. He said he was beginning to change his mind about the education of girls—he was amazed at the number of clever and well-educated 'English ladies' he had met. He said he did not know much about education, but I assured him that he knew a lot more than many English people. Both parents were genuinely interested and not merely in their own children.

(vi) *Summing-up*

This was a very long interview—three and a half hours—but a stimulating and useful one. It was good to view our schools from the viewpoint of an outsider. Mr Sakuntla was an intelligent and widely read man and very good company. His wife said the interview had helped to dispel some of her fears.

5.   VISIT TO MR & MRS JACKSON

(i) *General impression of home and parents*

There are five children, two girls and three boys, and the boys are all at our school. They live in a new council flat only a few minutes' walk from the school but despite this the boys are often late and the oldest is often away for no good reason. Tommy, the middle one, is nine. Sidney his older brother is eleven, and the youngest, Frank, is eight. The two girls are at secondary schools.

Sidney is a quiet boy, good at games and art. Tommy is the most definite character; big and strong for his age, aggressive and a real leader, but very retarded, especially in reading. Like his elder brother he is gifted at games, is a keen swimmer and footballer, has considerable skill at art and, unlike Sidney, loves acting and is a clever mime.

Frank is similar to Tommy with outbursts of aggressive behaviour but his abilities have not yet shown themselves and his class teacher describes him as 'often thwarted because his poor level of speech and reading prevents him doing as he wishes'.

Each of the boys has had over thirty half-day absences in the previous six months. I had discussed this before the interview with the other two class teachers (Tommy is in my class), with the head teacher and the school attendance officer.

(ii) *Main points covered in interview*

a. Mrs Jackson had been to the school occasionally, usually to discuss Tommy's aggressive behaviour or to explain why the boys had been truanting. The truanting had got to the stage where prosecution was being considered.

b. They said they did not really understand modern education but felt children had a much more interesting time at school today; they instanced swimming and games, drama, school journeys and excursions.

c. On discipline the main discussion took place. Mr Jackson said we did a good job keeping children in order. 'I know what our three perishers are like.' Mrs Jackson agreed that the boys were often away with no valid reason. They stayed up too late. 'I rue the day we brought that tele. But what can you do with five kids? This is a nice flat but not really big enough. The girls have to do their homework so the boys go out, then they get up to mischief.' Both parents agreed that as the boys were backward and found reading a struggle they resented school even though they found many of its activities interesting.

Mrs Jackson said she found it hard to show affection to the boys. 'I've never been one for kissing and cuddling them— I wonder if I've done right?'

Mrs Jackson did not work and had not for some years; she frankly said she knew she ought to be interested in what the children did but she was not and they resented this. I suggested that if they helped with the shopping and housework it would give her more time to relax with them.

(iii) *Information learnt*

Tommy had been knocked down by a car when he was six and had suffered concussion and a broken collar-bone. The hospital said he was quite recovered but his father said, 'He gets very bad-tempered and depressed; he isn't the same boy since.'

Mr Jackson had an electrical business and was often away from home.

That the three boys resented their older sisters.

(iv) *Problems discovered*

That the parents found it very difficult to control the children's T.V. viewing and the time they went to bed.

That the children roamed the neighbourhood until quite late at night, and that their father was often away from home.

(v) *Parents' attitudes to school and education*

Both were very friendly and grateful for the help the school gave. They promised to stop the boys truanting, calling them in while I was there and telling them firmly that they would in future go to school regularly.

This had a great effect—in the next six months their absences were very few. On one occasion Mrs Jackson called at the school with Frank whom she had found darting off to the park.

(vi) *Summing-up*

This was another long interview lasting nearly three hours, but most useful and with practical results. Not only was the truanting stopped but the boys' aggressive behaviour greatly reduced. Yet these parents are typical of many whom it is tempting to regard as apathetic and not worth helping.

G

CHAPTER 9

Prospects for the Future

'GETTING in to that school is like getting in to Buckingham Palace—and the headmistress is the Queen.'

This was the answer given to me by a father. I had advised him to take up with the head teacher a complaint that his son had had five teachers in the space of one term. His dilemma is typical of the feelings of many parents, particularly those in working class areas. He was concerned that his child should get a good education. He knew that there was a large turnover in staff at his son's school—it was in an area in London which had 'gone down' and the building was dark, old and very uninviting. Nearby was a Council estate with many modern features and facilities—playgrounds, a library, pubs, bright new shops, and a tenants' centre. Many of these facilities had been secured as the result of organisation and pressure. But to get a new school and a stable staff for it meant a different kind of organisation and pressure. The father concerned had felt few qualms in approaching councillors, MPs, or vicars in his work for the tenants. But teachers were, to him, rather more mysterious figures and, in an ill-defined way, more powerful. They commanded his child's loyalty in a much more concrete fashion than did the vicar or the MP.

Whether the headmistress did behave like a Queen or not was not really the point at issue. The father, like countless others, had no knowledge of how to approach the school and no confidence in being successful if he did.

Many Government reports have shown how children of working-class parents do not benefit from education as much

98

as middle-class children do. Crowther and Robbins showed that far too many bright working-class children, as well as the less able, left school at the earliest opportunity. In fact the Robbins Report demonstrated that a manual worker's child 'compared with the child of a non-manual worker' stood only one-seventh of the chance of getting to university in the decade before the war and, contrary to expectation, almost the same chance in the decade after the war.

Other evidence points to similar conclusions. For example, in J. W. B. Douglas's *The Home and the School,*[1] which is based on a study of the development of 5,000 children born in 1946, it is stated that in areas where grammar school places are provided for 20% or less of the children leaving primary schools children of lower manual working class parents get only 52% of the places expected from their ability, measured at eight years. Where more than 20% grammar places are provided they get 72% of the places expected. But children of upper middle class parents get virtually the same proportion of places, related to their ability, whether they live where grammar schools are generously provided or not!

So something happens between eight and eleven and for many working class children what happens is a *deterioration,* at least in measured ability.

Why is this, what has it to do with parents and teachers getting together and, as far as possible, working together— and can it be changed?

Douglas's findings, some of the evidence submitted to the Plowden Committee, and much of the evidence contained in this book seem to point to the same conclusion—that parents' *attitudes* towards their children's education are very important, perhaps decisively so, for educational success. This is not to say that working-class children do less well than expected because their parents don't care. There is little point in having

[1] J. W. B. Douglas: *The Home and the School* (MacGibbon and Kee, 1964)

an attitude towards a process you feel cannot affect; your attitude will be one of passivity and resignation.

J. B. Mays refers to this problem of the passivity of many working-class parents in the conclusions he draws from the Liverpool survey described in *Education and the Urban Child*.[2] Speaking of the 'downtown' areas, he writes:

'The residents of these localities, it must be admitted, have seldom been treated as anything more than second-class citizens for whom a substandard physical environment and inferior educational and other services have been regarded as adequate . . . Their presumable desire for higher status and better financial reward was in the past undeniably impeded by the general structure of our society which determined the role of such localities and, ipso facto, the social rank of their inhabitants. As a result of this, those who have been born and bred in such districts have inherited not only certain subcultural values but also the inferior status which other more favourable sections of the wider community have conferred upon them.'

Middle class parents know more about what they want from education. What they want may sometimes, in our view, be undesirable—perhaps even the antithesis of education in the sense of culture or of social responsibility. Yet they want it and know how to apply pressure to get what they want. Jackson and Marsden's *Education and the Working Class* makes this point:

'The schools usually offered an annual opportunity for parents to consult teachers, and of course it was always possible to make an appointment with the head. Yet it was clear indeed that these opportunities were only taken up by the more prosperous.'[3]

They can afford to pay for their children to be coached for

[2] J. B. Mays: *Education and the Urban Child*, pp 179-180.
[3] Jackson & Marsden: *Education and the Working Class*, p. 117.

the 11-plus. They can afford to move house so that their child can attend a particularly good school. That admirable and dynamic body, the Advisory Centre for Education, calls its magazine, 'Where?' The people who read it—and far too few working-class parents read it—have some choice in *where* they send their children to school.

I feel that it is important to help change the opinions of many articulate middle-class parents; opinions that streaming and competitiveness are good, that 'messing about with paint and music are a waste of time,' that it is all right that a class should be divided into the 'Very Goods', 'Goods', Try Hards', and 'Bads' which happens in a school in a middle-class district I know.

Middle-class competitiveness can be as bad as working-class apathy. Of course not all middle-class people are like this but when they are formed their attitudes are more difficult to. amend. Middle-class people are more articulate and more successful—they have been the successes of formal education, from the grammar schools. Too often they see educational success as the ability to pass examinations.

Working class attitudes are often distinctly different. Too often they are characterised by passive acceptance, an acceptance which has its origins in their own unhappy or at least unsatisfying experiences at school, sometimes the kind of schools criticised in the Newsom report, which in inadequate buildings in difficult areas were able to pay less attention than was necessary to personal development or social awareness because they had larger classes and less qualified staff.

Because we deplore and want to change the attitude of *some* working-class people in wanting to 'keep down with the Smiths' we should also not only deplore but try to change the attitude of *some* middle-class people expressed in the better-known phrase—'keeping up with the Jones's'.

To the middle-class the school is not a holy of holies nor the teaching profession high priests. Education is often regarded as an investment—the teachers are in charge of the balance-sheets which have to be readily available for inspection. The 'Education Shop' organised by the Advisory Centre for Education in Ipswich in October 1965 had posters announcing 'Every year at school after fifteen is worth £2,500 over a lifetime.' To the working class this is not so—or very much less so. Teachers are the experts. 'Well, you know all the answers, don't you? That's why you're teachers anyway,' one Mother said to me.

When working-class parents are given the opportunity to participate many do so with consequent benefit to their children—our experiment in a small school bore this out.

Can the present position be changed? Can the alarming wastage of ability, especially among working-class children, be stopped or diminished? It would be wrong to claim that the development of more co-operative relations between home and school could speedily solve this problem, yet more and more teachers are coming to see that such a development would at least help.

I feel it is the responsibility of teachers to help parents voice their feelings and wishes, to articulate more effectively, to know their way around the educational system as most middle class people do, and to use it actively instead of just accepting it. We teachers can do this by drawing parents in to the process of education, showing them how we teach and what they can do at home to reinforce this. We can make it clear that we regard parents as our allies. We can stress our readiness to *learn from them*. This means giving them the opportunity to tell us what they consider relevant facts not merely about their children but about their jobs, about the school environment, and about anything else which may be of use to the school. It is no use berating parents with the complaint 'They are only interested in their own child.' We should be thinking 'What opportunities can we give parents to be interested in something other than their own children?'

There are many ways in which we can draw parents into the daily life of the school. They can accompany teachers on educational excursions. They can make costumes for the school play. Their talents as cooks, electricians, painters, and gardeners could be used much more. Parents who are nurses, postmen, lorry-drivers, policemen, shopkeepers could talk about their jobs. Immigrant parents could talk about the customs of their people. This brings us to the vexed question of auxiliary and ancillary helpers.

The National Union of Teachers, of which I am a member, has quite rightly expressed its opposition to untrained teachers. Parents can help and, in fact, take part in the educational process, but to have them in charge of a class is not to help solve the teacher shortage but rather to perpetuate it.

If teachers are to try to alter the parents' attitudes then they must examine their own to see if they need alteration. Most teachers would consider it deplorable if a colleague criticised them in the hearing of children. Yet it is by no means rare to hear a teacher make sharply critical remarks about parents in children's hearing or directly to them. I can recall very many cases. In particular, a quite gifted teacher, who was also, incidentally, a parent, said to a child while I was present, 'Oh of course, we never get an answer from your parents, do we? They just can't be bothered.' This kind of remark, whatever has caused it, is quite inexcusable. It makes a child develop a quite unnecessary antagonism towards the school and, possibly, towards education in general.

Some teachers identify themselves very closely with children, recognising their potential. It is very disturbing for them to see that indifference or ignorance on the parents' part will nullify the effects of good teaching. And therefore it is tempting to try to make the child identify itself with the school, to make it rise above its family environment. Before the development of the comprehensive school it was infuriating for teachers to see parents turn down the offer of a grammar school place for their child for no good reason. This close identification of teachers with their pupils can be a danger. It can lead to a desire to fight the pupil's background. When I was a child I can well recall the resentment swelling up in me when our head-teacher told us once, in morning Assembly, 'You have come from the working class. It's the job of this school to move you out of that class.'

Teachers could usefully take stock of the opportunities they have for contact and co-operation with parents, to see how they can be used, developed, and improved. Parents could do the same. We live in a democratic society, but it only remains democratic if we really take advantage of it. Too few parents do. Too many accept seemingly arbitrary directives from schools; they grumble about them but do not challenge them or ask for information in a sensible way.

If teachers should refrain from criticising parents to the children then parents too should be careful what they say about teachers when children are listening. Too often parents take as gospel what children say about school, like the parent who wrote to me, 'From what I hear from other children the teachers have favourites.' When parents say to their children things like, 'Your teacher's talking out the back of his neck'— and I have heard this and many other such derogatory remarks —they are treading a dangerous path. Divided loyalties can arise in a child here, too. If teachers should make an imaginative effort to understand parents' difficulties in bringing children up, parents, in return, should try to understand the difficulties of the teacher's job. Further, they should try to convey this understanding.

I remember taking a party of children away for a fortnight for an educational trip. When we returned, after a fascinating but exhausting time, the parents were waiting outside the school. They pressed forward eagerly to greet their children. One, just one, came to me and said, 'It must have been a tough two weeks for you. We appreciate it very much. Thank you.'

Parents must overcome the feeling that if they are going to the school or speaking to the teachers their neighbours will think they are seeking special attention for their children. When a school offers the means for real contact parents have only themselves to blame if they do not respond. What is a teacher to think when only half the parents bother to come to an Open Evening?

As well as parents and teachers local education authorities have a responsibility in helping home and school to work in concert. Many authorities subscribe to this in theory; too few in detailed practice. Some education officers, for example in Nottinghamshire and in the West Riding, issue letters to parents—on sex education, smoking, television etc. Some organise parents' meetings, especially when some change in secondary education is proposed.

It would help if every LEA periodically reviewed the contacts schools have with parents, publicising the successes and analysing the failures. Jackson and Marsden suggest that local authorities provide a more permanent centre for answering parents' queries: 'The London Institute of Education successfully provides an Adviser to Teachers, supplementary to head masters and head mistresses. If an adviser to Teachers, why not an Adviser to Parents!'[4] It is said that it all depends on the teachers, that no decisive improvement is possible unless they re-think their attitudes towards parents. In one sense this is true. Education authorities can encourage, even exhort, but teachers, who have the day-to-day contact with parents, can act.

Like any other advance in education the one we hope for here will have to be paid for. In crude terms, the most antipathetic group of teachers would be unlikely to maintain their opposition to co-operation with parents if they were given an extra teacher to help, or if they were entitled to a morning off after an evening interview with parents.

[4] *Op Cit.*, p. 208.

There are many dedicated teachers ready to accept the burdens—and they can be heavy ones—of working with parents. Can we rely on the dedicated ones? I feel not, any more than we can rely on dedicated nurses to maintain our hospitals, accepting grossly inadequate wages for doing vital work.

Local authorities have to allocate finance for education. It is the Government who authorise it and in the long run, in our democratic process, this means the responsibility comes back to us all. How much money are we going to spend, and how are we going to spend it? It is not for teachers alone to say.

If it is true—and it obviously is—that the attitudes of teachers are all-important in making a decisive improvement in home-school relations, then it follows that the institutions responsible for training teachers have a great responsibility.

The training colleges—or Colleges of Education as they are now called—receive students in their late teens or early twenties, for the most part. University Institutes of Education take graduates who are a few years older, for a shorter course. How many of these institutions deal with parent-teacher relations in their courses? How often is it pointed out to students that the children they teach are the products of a particular environment which is of considerable relevance in the classroom? Or, when some attempt is made to grapple with this problem, how often are students thwarted by lack of time and by detailed guidance on how to study the environment and in particular the parents?

J. B. Mays's survey of Liverpool schools, to which reference has been made already, reveals that many of the class teachers felt cut off from the children by cultural differences:

'They suggested that training colleges should spend some time acquainting them during student days with different types of social background and introduce them to such simple and generally useful sociological topics as social stratification, the existence of sub-cultures and the various patterns of behaviour associated with them.'[5]

From my own experience I would say that few student teachers are given such guidance, and I have personally supervised the teaching practice of students from a dozen colleges. It is argued that most students in training are not parents themselves, and in any case are not mature enough to grapple with the social and emotional problems which experienced teachers find difficult. One could answer that many teachers are not parents either, and that an immature student will not develop into a mature one without some practical experience of a social character.

It has been implied throughout this book, and often stated, that teachers do their job much more effectively if they try to work with rather than against the parents and the environment. It is beginning to be understood that teachers are not merely givers of knowledge. They are, or should be, ready to learn more and more about the children they teach. To learn from the children, from their parents, from the community or neighbourhood round the school means that teachers must look again at their own rôle, must see it as a dual rôle, leading children to acquire knowledge and good attitudes to learning and social responsibility and also reaching out beyond the child to influence the attitudes of those who have reared the child. Much mistrust and many cherished notions held by teachers will have to be re-examined, re-appraised and some of them, perhaps, abandoned in this process.

In this connection, too, J. B. Mays has some challenging things to say:

'The duality of the teacher's role seems inescapable and any refusal on the part of the profession to accept the reality of the situation will result in the ultimate deprivation and disadvantage of their scholars. For this reason it seems to be of paramount importance that a strong link should be created

[5] J. B. Mays: *Education and the Urban Child*, p. 115.

between school and home, and that teachers should make every possible endeavour to secure an adequate working relationship with parents. This may not involve the organisation of a formal association, but, whatever form it takes, the distrust and timidity which at present characterise the attitude of many teachers towards collaboration with the home are major obstacles in the way of progress. Moreover, the plea of parochial schools that they are already sufficiently integrated into the general life of the neighbourhood is manifestly lacking in foundation.'[6]

Teaching *is* social work, in the sense that children cannot be effectively educated in isolation from their background. This truth is slowly gaining acceptance. For example, Edge Hill College of Education at Ormskirk, near Liverpool, is training 'teacher social workers,' who will eventually 'take up appointments involving responsibility for a variety of contacts with parents and local social workers.'

I quote here from the challenging and altogether praiseworthy prospectus of the Edge Hill College:

'The course also offers studies in the techniques of parent-teacher contact, and introductions to such skills as remedial teaching which will be of direct classroom relevance later.'

It used to be said that 'every teacher is a teacher of English.' We ought to be saying now that 'every teacher is a social worker.' Unfortunately the example of Edge Hill has found few followers elsewhere. The problem of training enough teachers is a complex one. On its solution depends much of our future. If we are going to solve it there seems to be little doubt that we will have to attract far more students in the thirty to fifty age range. Working with parents, understanding the significance of home background should present much less difficulty to such students. Many are parents themselves, with experience of the world outside the school or college circle. I have had the privilege of working with many such students,

[6] *Op cit.*, p. 190.

especially those from Sidney Webb College in London, and found them quick to see the need for studying the attitudes of parents and relating the shape and sound and smell of the neighbourhood to the day-to-day life of the classroom. It is no criticism of the twenty-year-old student-teacher to say that a big expansion of the numbers of more mature students would not only help solve the shortage but would also be a significant advance in the field of parent-teacher communication.

What is being done to make the parent-teacher dialogue more effective? Mention has already been made of the Advisory Centre for Education, and its intriguing and original 'Education Shop' experiment. The experiment consisted of taking space in the main store of the Ipswich Co-operative Society for a week in October 1965, for an exhibition on education and, more important, for a centre at which parents, and others, could ask questions, seek information, or raise educational problems.

ACE does what it may be thought most local education authorities should or could do. Education badly needs public relations; ACE and its magazine 'Where?' is an unofficial, and unsubsidized, public relations officer for the education system, providing a forum for parents and a platform for teachers.

The Education Shop experiment was designed to see if there was a demand for information about schools which was not being satisfied through the 'usual channels'. There *was* such an unsatisfied demand; in the six days when the 'shop' was open and its panel of advisors on duty 225 people came with problems, many more visited the accompanying exhibition, and there were follow-up interviews with 93 parents.

The local education office seemed very inaccessible to some. One parent said, 'You're made to feel your child's just a cog in the wheel.' Many thought the education office was open only to teachers. Another said, 'I've wanted to find out things about education, but you don't like to make an appointment. You feel you're on trial yourself.'

Some parents who had gone to their child's school with a problem had come away dissatisfied. Others felt too diffident to go. 'You can't demand. If you make a fuss, they take it out on the child.'

The report on the 'shop' recommends more such ventures, preferably run by local education authorities, and makes the point that parents need an opportunity to talk freely about their children to an informed and sympathetic listener. It also points out that parents need an independent source of advice in cases where they feel a child has been unfairly treated or under-estimated. I personally think that it is the *school's* function to act as an independent source of advice; where further arbitration is needed something has already gone wrong; the lines of communication have broken down.

A most important conclusion of the report was that the failure of schools to communicate with many parents who are interested in their child's education is holding back many children, especially working class children, and is causing a great wastage of ability.

The work of Michael Young and Patrick McGeeney has also done much to stimulate teachers to think anew about how to work with parents. The researches initiated by the Institute of Community Studies at Bethnal Green have encouraged many who have begun to consider new approaches to parents and have reinforced the faith—and it is faith— of the few who had already begun to experiment on their own.

In London a few gifted and determined head teachers have made independent and original attempts to reach out and involve parents—Harry Stephenson in Bethnal Green and Eltham, David Mackay in St Pancras, and Peter Bensley in Plumstead. Basically these head teachers have begun by asking the parents what kind of contact *they* want, by reviewing the points at which contact is already being made and deciding, with the facilities of the school and the attitudes of teachers taken into consideration, which is the most profitable avenue to pursue.

At the Gordon Primary School in Eltham, Stephenson used a questionnaire divided into two sections, 'How can the School help you?' and 'How can you help the School?' Parents were asked if they would like an 'Open Evening' each year as well as an 'Open Day'; 86% said Yes'. Asked if they would like to hear an occasional talk on educational topics, 85% answered 'Yes'. 94% said they would like a private interview with the Head.

A most important finding was that nine of of every ten parents tried to help children with school work and would welcome information on how to do so more effectively.

Large numbers of parents were willing to help the school in a variety of ways: covering books and cataloguing, making toys and apparatus, looking after children on outings, typing, running jumble sales, helping with the school garden, and so on.

At this school Stephenson is applying the fruit of considerable experience in a rather different school, Hague Primary in Bethnal Green. There in a closely-knit working-class community the school played a real and valuable role and one which aroused the interest of sociologists and teachers alike. Born in South Shields in the early 'twenties Harry Stephenson is the kind of head teacher who can talk to and win the confidence of parents, both working-class and middle-class.

Stephenson writes with great insight about the changes in his ideas on parent-teacher co-operation, changes prompted by his desire to know more about the education of his own two children:

'As a Head of about three years standing I felt reasonably satisfied with the progress my school had made in the sphere of parental co-operation—I had taken down a notice on the

Head's door "Parents seen only at the following times or by appointment", I had introduced an Open Evening in place of an Open Day so that father and working mothers could come along to the school to see the children's work and to consult the class teacher. I started issuing the standard L.C.C. report forms for Junior children, so that parents could have more detailed information about their children's progress. I made myself available to parents whenever they came up to school to discuss some problem or to make a complaint. These measures had brought my school, so I believed, into line with most schools considered progressive in this sphere.

At the same time, however, I was becoming increasingly dissatisfied, as a parent and ratepayer, with the educational service my children were receiving at their primary school. As a ratepayer I was not happy about the local provisions for Secondary education and about overcrowding in the Primary schools. As a parent I found myself unaware of what my children were doing in school or of the progress they were making. I felt in great need of information about my children —what the school thought of them, what they thought about the school, what relationships had my children with their schoolfellows and with their teacher, what difficulties were they encountering in their school work, had they any specific weaknesses, what was the teachers opinion of their character and personality, what sort of teaching were they getting, what were the causes of emotional difficulties which were occasionally in evidence at home and seemed to emanate from school experiences, why were they transferred from one stream to another—these and many other questions troubled my mind. On the occasion of the annual Open Evening, similar to those held at my own school, I would visit the school, where an extensive exhibition of work was the main feature of the Evening. Amid the piles of exercise books, models, needlework and art exhibits, repeated in every classroom and overflowing into corridors and hall, sat the class teacher, tense and apprehensive, awaiting the onrush of eager questioning parents, fearing the arrival of a critical or angry parent, and hoping that soon the time would arrive when she could pack up and go home, her ordeal over. On such visits I would make a perfunctory survey of the display material, experiencing the occasional glow of pleasure at sight of contributions made by my own children, yet spurred on and beyond by the nagging uncertainties and questions within me. I therefore always made a point of edging towards the teacher keeping an alert eye on those parents already engaging her attention. Pausing only to scan the long lists of subject and class positions and examination results—never, for me, a very uplifting experience—I would arrive finally before the teacher: — "Mr Stephenson?— oh yes! the twins—very nice children—getting along very well —very alike aren't they?—satisfactory progress—nothing to worry about—and now if you'll excuse me I have another parent waiting . . . " My few minutes were up. Each year, the snippets of information gleaned at Open Evenings gave me less and less satisfaction, until finally I sought an interview with the headmaster. My request was granted and I was received in a friendly and co-operative manner, although I am uncertain as to what extent this was due to my being a member of the teaching profession. Moreover the head made clear in his view that parents should leave everything to the school and that "as long as children were happy there was nothing to worry about." He did not make clear how he discovered whether a child was happy or not, but seemed convinced that *all* the children in his school were happy and therefore, according to his philosophy, no further contact with parents was necessary apart from the annual Open Evening. No further contact, that is in the educational sphere, for there was in existence a thriving PTA which had raised £2,000 for a swimming pool by means of whist drives, dances, fêtes, draw tickets etc.

As I took stock of my experiences as a parent, it begun to

113

dawn upon me that I was adopting in my school (the Hague) precisely the same attitudes as that headmaster! I started to ask myself whether there were parents of children at the Hague who felt as dissatisfied, anxious and helpless about their children's education as I did about my own children's. How could I reconcile my feeling of satisfaction at what I was doing as a head with my feeling of discontent as a parent of children attending a school run on identical lines to mine? There began to develop in me a growing awareness of the need for closer and more frequent contacts between school and parents; and yet there were still doubts in my mind regarding the conclusions I was beginning to draw from this conflict of ideas. Might not closer contact with parents to relieve their anxieties and doubts simply transfer these to the children, thrusting them more into the limelight and making them more conscious of success or failure? Would teachers become exposed to uninformed criticism from parents and to interference and pressures which would make their work more difficult? The first of these doubts was allayed very quickly, again as a result of my children's educational development. By this time they had embarked upon their Secondary education and quite by chance, as a result of community service work, I became well acquainted with the Head of their Secondary School and had frequent discussions about my children's work and progress, their difficulties and problems. I made frequent visits to the school, learnt a great deal about the educational environment my children were experiencing and about the policy of the school. My children were aware of this closer contact but, instead of becoming more intense and over-anxious, they became more relaxed and self-confident and made greater progress than had been anticipated at the time of their transfer to Secondary education. Part of this change was probably due to growing maturity, but I was convinced that it was also due partly to this closer contact between school and home. Moreover, in addition to having my doubts

114

and anxieties resolved and my need for information satisfied, I came to the conclusion that parental interest and co-operation with schools could also have a significant bearing upon children's educational progress.

With regard to the second of my doubts—whether teachers would be apprehensive about uninformed parental criticism and possible pressures—it seemed best to hold a series of Staff meetings and discussions before deciding to proceed further. One conclusion arising from these discussions was that if there was to be parental criticism it should be informed criticism and that one function of parent-school co-operation should be to explain modern educational ideas to parents and to show them what we were trying to do in school. If this were done, in fact, critical attitudes might disappear altogether.'

At de Lucy Junior School in Plumstead Peter Bensley inherited a PTA but has also involved parents in many new ways. He, too, used a questionnaire to find out what the parents wanted—and what they would *give*. As a result he planned meetings designed to explain to parents the new ways of learning mathematics, physical education, music etc. These meetings were very successful. The photographs in the local press of mothers and fathers sitting at a desk while a very young teacher—or even a child—demonstrated the use of Cuisenaire rods, speak volumes for the value of this approach!

Bensley also experimented with having parents helping on the building while school was in progress, even working in the classroom under the direction of the class teacher: in the library, making apparatus, and helping with construction work such as the building of climbing frames and aviaries. Another valuable method of enlisting the aid of the parents in actual lessons has been to invite mothers and fathers to talk to the children about hobbies, jobs, or interesting places.

David Mackay is another who has been a pioneer in the field of home-school relations. In two city schools with widely contrasting backgrounds he investigated a number of new and very successful ways of reaching out to and involving parents. His starting point was the need to explain modern ideas on teaching methods and discipline which were often very different from those experienced by the parents in their own school careers.

As a result of such work a few other schools are beginning tentatively to review and extend their contacts with parents, local authorities and their school inspectors are holding conferences on the home and the school, and advertisements for teachers are seen couched in such terms as: 'Deputy Head wanted for this school. Interest in taking part in new methods of parent-teacher relations essential'.

Original work is not confined to London teachers of course. A. W. Rowe at David Lister School in Hull, S. W. Percival in Oxfordshire, John Hunt in Havant, and others, have made successful efforts to work with parents, to involve them in the life of the school, and to reach out to the neighbourhood. John Bellis, head of a Blackpool Junior school, is with Peter Bensley one of the very few to have a teacher-social worker on his staff. Bellis is not satisfied with the school being 'outward looking'—he feels it should be 'outward going'. And his school is precisely this. The teacher social worker visits homes in the evening (by appointment of course) and this work is part of the conditions of employment.

The organisation which most people think of when they hear of parent-teacher co-operation is the PTA. It has already been said that there will be no significant advance in this field until there are many more PTAs. The movement is still in its early days—the English National Federation of PTAs has been in existence only since 1956, though it carries on the work of the Home and School Council and the 1944 Committee for Parent-Teacher Organisation. The English Federation does much valuable work, issuing a magazine and holding an annual conference. There is no national membership; individuals are members of a local PTA; but in 1961 only 550 such groups were federated. It is clear that, while no direct comparison of English and American experience is possible, the organised movement for co-operation is much older, more powerful, and more widespread in the USA. (The American National Congress of Parents and Teachers was founded in 1897, has a membership of *thirteen million,* and its magazine, the *National Parent-Teacher* has a seven-figure circulation. It maintains a massive full-time staff, in contrast to the English Federation which has no full-time paid officials.)

All this is no criticism of the work of the English PTA movement. Here as in many fields of social work too much is being done by too few.

Yet a feeling common to many teachers who are pioneering new developments—and to many parents—is that the setting up of a PTA does not solve anything. How do we avoid the PTA committee being dominated by middle-class articulates, how do we reach the 'problem' parents who shun meetings, and how do we get beyond the stage of raising money for a swimming pool? How also is the stage reached when the PTA can organise parents to take part in the daily *educational* work of the school—for this is the next step.

Parents want to discuss, and should be discussing, the initial teaching alphabet, science in the junior school, television, rewards and punishments, religious education, the teaching of reading, streaming, juvenile delinquency, sex education. Parents are vitally concerned in these subjects. Because they affect their children they are even more vitally concerned than the teachers. And of course they *do* discuss. They talk among themselves. And they act as well. They try to teach their children to read, and often succeed. They try to understand the 'new mathematics', they help their children's projects. All too often, even with a PTA, they never talk to the teachers about such subjects. When they do it is usually as individual parents, and this is good. But with the sweeping changes of emphasis and method in the last decade—especially in the primary, secondary modern and comprehensive schools —there is an overwhelming case for making discussions, on what is taught and how it is being taught, organised and systematic.

How can we get the best out of our schools when parents taught to read by phonic methods are trying to help children who are learning by 'look and say'? Or, more important still, when parents who were caned daily know, but don't understand why, the cane is never used on their children?

In many areas parents who want to co-operate with teachers but find there is no PTA at their child's school have joined a local branch of AASE—Associations for the Advancement of State Education. These bodies have a rather different emphasis; they are designed to act as local pressure groups to campaign for smaller classes, better school buildings, indoor toilets etc. (In this connection the following exchanges from *Hansard* for November 17, 1966, are appropriate and show what great problems are to be overcome, problems which are hardly likely to be more than nibbled at while teachers and parents work separately.)

Dr J. Dunwoody asked the Secretary of State for Education and Science in what number and in what percentage of primary schools in Cornwall, and in England as a whole, is there outdoor sanitation.

Mr Redhead: The only comparative figures available are those compiled in 1962 which showed 256 such schools (90%) in Cornwall, and 13,810 (66%) in England. The current figure for Cornwall is 228 schools (83%).

Dr J. Dunwoody asked in what number and in what percentage of primary schools in Cornwall and England as a whole does the oldest main building date from 1902 or earlier.

Mr Redhead: The only comparative figures available are those compiled in 1962 which showed 220 such schools (77%) in Cornwall and 12,566 (60%) in England.'

CONCLUSIONS

If this book stimulates only a few parents and teachers to act, to look again at the opportunities they have of meeting and working constructively together, it will have been worth writing. Parents and teachers are not enemies; they should not be rivals even but partners. There could be no more fitting way to end a book addressed to them both than to remind them of the methods by which they can reinforce each other's work and to suggest some new methods.

WHAT CAN PARENTS DO?

1. *Offer whatever help you can to the school.* It is the thought which counts and many schools, especially the smaller ones, are perpetually short of money. Discarded toys and books, money for school fund, dressing-up clothes, magazines, games for wet dinner-times, flowers for assembly; these can lead the way to such things as accompanying school outings, giving talks at the school, organising jumble sales or fetes.

2. *Join the PTA or Parents' Association.* Take a more active part if you are already a member; try to help form at PTA if there isn't one. And/or join or help form a local AASE.

3. *Write or telephone your thanks* if your child is getting on well or is being given extra facilities, such as Saturday morning football, school journey, educational excursions. Make it clear that you appreciate this voluntary work. Ask if you can help with it in any way.

4. *Reply to school reports.* Ask for clarification if necessary; give *your* view of your child. If you feel grateful *say so!* Say what kind of report you would like.

119

5. *Ask to see the head or class teacher.* Do this if you feel it will help the school—and the child. Find out how you can help your child at home. Do not be afraid to invite the head or the teacher for a talk at your home—he can only say 'no'! Attend school functions whenever you can.

6. *Remember the teachers' point of view;* Your child may be a very different personality at school.

a. Parent-teacher co-operation *should not* make life more difficult for teachers; this may largely depend on you, the parent.

b. Do not grumble about school in front of children.

c. The teachers are struggling against enormous difficulties— overlarge classes, out-of-date buildings, inadequate facilities. Make it clear that you know this and are trying to do something about it, by letters to the Press, through your Trade Union or political party etc.

7. *Lastly,* do not just worry or grouse about your child at school. Act; ask for information, and advise other parents to do the same.

WHAT CAN TEACHERS DO?

1. *Review the contacts* you have with parents. Do they work; how many parents do you never see? Is this number irreducible?

2. PTAs. Why not take the lead in forming one? They do not have to be like the ones you hear about in the USA! They can, at their best, be the most developed and organised way of stimulating real co-operation. Even at their worst they have something to offer, and a poor organisation can be made into a good one.

3. *School reports.* These could do with a re-appraisal. There are many schools which are successfully using modern methods—and communicating to parents about the results on forms which 'came out of the ark'. Some schools have done

away with reports, which is throwing out the baby with the bath water. Has your school report any point at all in its present form?

4. *The neighbourhood.* It is worth wandering round the back streets, or in and out of the Council flats, and it is surprising how many teachers do not. If you are recognised by children and parents so much the better. Standing in the same queue at the co-op puts many problems in proportion. In this way you become part of the neighbourhood, not just part of the school.

5. *Talking to parents,* or rather talking *with* parents. As a sympathetic listener you are worth your weight in gold. Few people confide in a minister of religion. For many people, especially working-class mothers, the school is literally the one place where they can talk and be listened to.

6. *Home visits.* These can be very rewarding, and very enjoyable. Ask your parents if you can come and have a chat. Parents we considered hostile and aggressive jumped at the chance. Such visits can completely alter, for the better, one's relations with a child.

7. *Remember the parents' point of view.* We try to see things through the child's eyes; it is a logical, and valuable, step to try now to see through the parents'. Much of our work is wasted if they are hostile, indifferent, or just plain puzzled. And when we stop learning from parents we stop learning altogether.

Useful organisations

1 National Federation of Parent Teacher Associations, 75 Primrose Hill Court, King Henry's Road, London, NW3. (01 722-9370).

2 Confederation of Associations for the Advancement of State Education, Mr G. Somerset, 42 Meadow Hill Road, Kings Norton, Birmingham 30.

3 Advisory Centre for Education, 57 Russell Street, Cambridge. Cambridge 51456.

4 National Union of Teachers, Hamilton House, Mabledon Place, London, WC1. EUSton 2442.

5 Comprehensive Schools Committee, 209 Belsize Road, London, NW6.

6 Nursery School Association of Great Britain & Ireland, 89 Stamford Street, London, SE1. WATerloo 7454.

7 National Foundation for Educational Research in England and Wales, 79 Wimpole Street, London, W1. WELbeck 8335.

8 National Child Development Study, 1958, Adam House, 1 Fitzroy Square, London, W1. EUSton 4263.

9 Home and School Council, 57 Russell Street, Cambridge. (Director—Sonia Abrams).

Suggestions for further reading

A. C. E.: *The Education Shop,*   A. C. E., Cambridge, 1966

Acland, R.: *We Teach them Wrong,*   Routledge & Kegan Paul, 1963

Blishen, E.: *Roaring Boys,*   Thames & Hudson, 1966

Bowlby, J.: *Child Care and the Growth of Love,*   Penguin, 1953

Braithwaite, E. R.: *To Sir, with Love,*   Bodley Head, 1959

Buhler, C.: *Childhood Problems and the Teacher,*   Routledge & Kegan Paul, 1953

Children and Their Primary Schools, Plowden Report   H.M.S.O., 1967

Craft, M. and others: *Linking Home and School,*   Longmans, Green, 1967

Cole, R.: *Comprehensive Schools in Action,*   Oldbourne Press, O/P

Daniels, J. C. and Diack, H.: *Learning to Read,*   Chatto & Windus, 1954

Douglas, J. W. B.: *Home and School,*   MacGibbon & Kee, 1964

Floud, T., Halsey, A. H., & Martin, F. M.: *Social Class and Educational Opportunity,*   Heinemann, 1957

Fraser, E.: *Home Environment and the School,*   University of London Press, 1959

Furneaux, R.: *The Chosen Few,*   Oxford University Press, O/P

Gardner, D.: *Experiment and Tradition in Primary School,*   Methuen, 1966

Hadfield, J. A.: *Childhood and Adolescence,*   Penguin, 1967

Hoggart, R.: *Uses of Literacy,*   Penguin, 1957

Hostler, P.: *The Child's World,*   Penguin, 1967

James, H. E. O., & Tenen, C.: *The Teacher was Black*   Heinemann, 1953

Jackson, B. & Marsden, D.: *Education and the Working Class,*   Penguin, 1966

Jackson, B.: *Streaming,*   Routledge & Kegan Paul, 1964

Lassell, M.: *Wellington Road,*   Penguin, 1966

Appendix B

Marshall, S.: *Experiment in Education,* Cambridge University Press, 1963

Mays, J. B.: *Education and the Urban Child,* Liverpool University Press, 1962

Mays, J. B.: *Growing up in the City,* Liverpool University Press, 1964

Mays, J. B.: *On the Threshold of Delinquency,* Liverpool University Press, 1959

Newson, J. & E.: *Patterns of Infant Care,* Penguin, 1965

Newton, K. & Abrams, S.: *Opportunities after 'O' Level,* Penguin, 1965

Opie, I. & P.: *Language and Lore of Schoolchildren,* Oxford University Press, 1959

Pedley, R.: *The Comprehensive School,* Penguin, 1967

P. E. P.: *Parents' View on Education,* P. E. P., 1961

Pringle, M. L. G.: *Deprivation and Education,* Longmans, Green, 1965

Report of the Committee on Maladjusted Children, H.M.S.O., 1955

Rowe, A.: *Education of the Average Child,* Harrap, 1959

Segal, C.: *Backward Children in the Making,* Muller, 1949

Simon, B.: *Intelligence Testing and the Comprehensive School,* Lawrence & Wishart, 1953

Simon, B.: *Studies in the History of Education,* Lawrence & Wishart, 1965

Stern, H. H.: *Parent Education,* University of Hull, 1960

Stott, D. H.: *Saving Children from Delinquency,* University of London Press, 1952

Tudor-Hart, B.: *Learning to Live,* Thames & Hudson, 1960

Vaizey, J.: *Education for Tomorrow,* Penguin, 1966

Valentine, C. W.: *The Normal Child and Some of his Abnormalities,* Penguin, 1967

Vernon, P. E.: *Secondary School Selection,* Methuen, 1957

Wilson, J.: *Public Schools and Private Practice,* Allen & Unwin, 1962

Young, M. & Willmott, P.: *Family and Kinship in East London,* Penguin, 1957

American books on home-school relationships

Note: A short list of American books is given here, most of them not published in England but available at libraries in University departments, etc. They are listed here because, of the forty-five English books suggested for further reading, only eighteen deal specifically with parent-teacher relations.

Baldwin, S. E., & Osborne, E. G.: *Home-school relations: Philosophy and practice,* Progressive Education Assn, New York, 1935

Baruch, D. W.: *Parents and teachers go to school,* Scott, Foreman & Co. Chicago 1939

D'Evelyn, K.: *Individual Parent-Teacher Conferences,* Teacher's College, Columbia University, New York, 1954

Hand, H. C.: *What People Think About Their Schools,* World Book Co. New York, 1948

Hymes, J. L.: *Effective Home-school Relations,* Prentice Hall, New York, 1953

Jersild, A. T.: *Joys and Problems of Child Rearing,* Teachers' College, Columbia University, New York, 1949

Jersild, A. T.: *In Search of Self,* Teachers' College, Columbia, University, New York, 1952

Jersild, A. T.: *Child Psychology,* Staples Press, New York, 1947

Jersild, A. T.: *When Teachers Face Themselves,* Teachers' College, Columbia University, New York, 1955

Langdon, G. and Stout, I. W.: *Helping Parents Understand Their Child's School,* Prentice Hall, New Jersey, 1957

Langdon, G., and Stout, I. W.: *Teacher-Parent Interviews,* Prentice Hall, New Jersey, 1957

Levy, D. M.: *Maternal Overprotection,* Columbia University Press, New York, 1943

Osborne, E.: *The Parent-Teacher Partnership,* Teachers' College, Columbia University, New York, 1959

Rogers, C. R.: *The Clinical Treatment of the Problem Child,* Houghton Mifflin, Boston 1939

Appendix C

Rohrer, J. H. and Sherif, M.: *Social Psychology at the Crossroads,* — Harper & Row, New York, 1951

Strang, R.: *Reporting to Parents,* — Teachers' College, Columbia University, New York, 1954

Strang, R.: *Educational Guidance: Principles and Practice,* — Macmillan, New York, 1948

Strang, R.: *Every Teacher's Records,* — Teachers' College, Columbia University, New York, 1947

The Parent-Teacher Organisation. Its Origins and Development, — National Congress of Parents and Teachers, Chicago, 1944

Index

Index